Pacific Reef and Shore

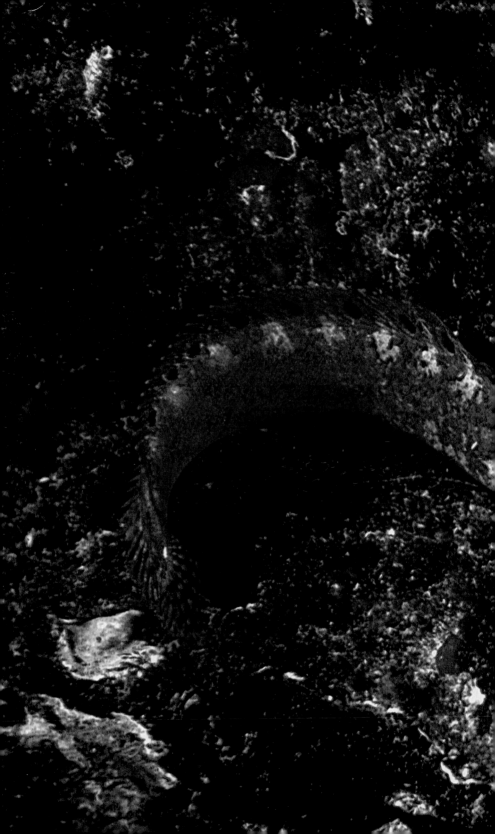

Pacific Reef and Shore

A Photo Guide to Northwest Marine Life
Revised Second Edition

Rick M. Harbo

HARBOUR
PUBLISHING

2 3 4 5 6 — 25 24 23 22 21

Harbour Publishing Co. Ltd.
P.O. Box 219, Madeira Park, BC, V0N 2H0
www.harbourpublishing.com

Cover design by Brianna Cerkiewicz
Text design by Roger Handling
Printed and bound in Canada

Harbour Publishing Co. Ltd. acknowledges the support of the Canada Council for the Arts, which last year invested $153 million to bring the arts to Canadians throughout the country. We also gratefully acknowledge financial support from the Government of Canada through the Canada Book Fund and from the Province of British Columbia through the BC Arts Council and the Book Publishing Tax Credit.

Library and Archives Canada Cataloguing in Publication

Harbo, Rick M., 1949-, author
 Pacific reef & shore : a photo guide to Northwest marine life / Rick M. Harbo. — Revised second edition.

Includes index.
Issued in print and electronic formats.
ISBN 978-1-55017-786-2 (softcover).—ISBN 978-1-55017-787-9 (HTML)

 1. Reef organisms—British Columbia—Pacific Coast—Identification. 2. Reef organisms—Pacific Coast (U.S.)—Identification. 3. Seashore animals—British Columbia—Pacific Coast—Identification. 4. Seashore animals—Pacific Coast (U.S.)—Identification. 5. Seashore plants—British Columbia—Pacific Coast—Identification. 6. Seashore plants—Pacific Coast (U.S.)—Identification. I. Title. II. Title: Pacific reef and shore.

QH95.3.H36 2017   578.769'909795   C2017-900898-6
                                                 C2017-900899-4

This book is dedicated to my family: Heather, Jennifer, Michael and Amy, and to my many friends who provided their assistance and shared their love and knowledge of the sea.

Acknowledgements

Scientific editing and advice were generously provided by numerous experts in the development of this guide. My thanks to Neil McDaniel, Ronald L. Shimek, William C. Austin, Claudia Mills, Daphne Fautin, Paul V. Scott, Eugene V. Coan, James McLean, Roger N. Clark, Sandra Millen, Karin Fletcher, Roland Anderson, Gregory Jensen, William Merilees, Philip Lambert, Gretchen Lambert, Charles Lambert, Andy Lamb, Graham Gillespie, Graeme Ellis, John Ford, Jane Watson, Jim Borrowman, Michael Hawkes, Sandra Lindstrom, Heidi Gartner and Duane Sept.

Special thanks to the editor, Mary Schendlinger, for giving clarity to the descriptions, and to copyeditor Merrie-Ellen Wilcox and proofreader Patricia Wolfe. Vici Johnstone provided valuable direction in the development of this guide. Mary White scanned photographs. Brianna Cerkiewicz prepared the index. Martin Nichols, Lionheart Graphics, contributed his talents to the design of the map on page 7, and Roger Handling, Terra Firma Digital Arts, designed the book's interior.

Contents

Northeast Pacific Ocean and Coast

ARCTIC OCEAN

Aleutian Islands

AK

GULF OF ALASKA

NORTH

Haida Gwaii

PACIFIC

BC

Vancouver Island

OCEAN

PUGET SOUND

WA

NORTH AMERICA

OR

N

CA

Point Conception

0   400

Kilometres

Region covered in this book

Baja

MX

Introduction

Thousands of fascinating creatures inhabit the beaches, tidepools and waves of the Pacific Northwest, and more than 300 species of marine animals and plants listed in this field guide are just those most commonly seen along the coast of Alaska, British Columbia, Washington, Oregon and northern California. Wonderful surprises await anyone—from the first-time beachcomber to the seasoned scuba diver—who spends an afternoon looking closely at the wildlife of our marine shores and waters.

Tides and Currents

Whether you are boating, diving or just walking along the seashore, you must be aware of the tides and currents in the area you are exploring. The earth's waters rise and recede, drawn by the gravitational pull of the moon, and to a lesser extent the sun. Tidal changes can be extreme, with a daily range in water height or depth of as much as 20′ (6 m) in some locations. Tidal changes also cause swift currents at narrows where water flow is constricted. Tide and current tables, published by government agencies, are available online, at marinas, and sporting goods stores.

The best time to view marine life is during the two hours before and after the lowest tide, generally less than 2′ (60 cm) in the USA and less than 3′ (1 m) in Canada. If you are an experienced diver and you plan to visit current-swept areas for the rich marine life, plan your dives for slack times, as the tides change direction.

The intertidal area of the beach is the part that is submerged at high tide and exposed at low tide, a habitat where many animals and plants are covered and uncovered by water twice a day. Creatures that live here are adapted to the high, mid- and/or low intertidal zones. The subtidal area is the shallow water, that part of the salt water that is within diving range (less than 100′/30 m deep). Species here are always submerged, and they live in conditions of much less rugged surf and exposure to weather than intertidal dwellers.

Names of Species

Almost every plant and animal has a common name, usually local and often colourful, such as the northwest ugly clam. The scientific name (*Entodesma navicula* for the northwest ugly clam), is a unique name composed of two words and registered with an international organization, gives scientists a standard, precise way of communicating information about a particular organism.

Scientific classifications and names are constantly under review as more is learned about wildlife, and species names change frequently, so there are often many synonyms for a given plant or animal. Many names have been updated in this second edition. Search the World Registry of Marine Species (WoRMS) for current accepted names and synonyms, http://www.marinespecies.org.

Marine Conservation

This guidebook is intended to help you identify animals and plants in their habitat without having to collect or otherwise disturb them. That is the best way to understand the relationships between organisms and their environment, and to protect them for future generations to observe and enjoy.

If you must take specimens, be aware of local Fisheries regulations and licensing requirements. Wherever possible, collect organisms from man-made structures such as docks and pilings. Take as few specimens as possible and avoid individuals that are laying or guarding eggs, or engaged in reproductive behaviours. If you dig into sand or mud, or turn over rocks, replace the disturbed material carefully and immediately. Avoid stepping on plants and animals.

There are many threats to the marine environment, including overfishing, pollution and habitat destruction. Many local or international marine conservation groups are active, and they will be glad to provide you with more information on enjoying and caring for the natural wonders of the coastline.

Marine Mammals
Whales, Dolphins, Porpoises, Seals & Sea Lions, Sea Otter & River Otter
Phylum Chordata

Illustrations by Pieter Folkens

Whales, Dolphins, Porpoises

Harbour Porpoise

Phocoena phocoena

To 6′3″ (1.8 m) long. Weight to 145 lb. (65 kg). Low, triangular dorsal fin. Small rounded head. Dark back, light sides to white, speckled belly. Solitary or in pairs, in coastal areas year-round. Avoids vessels; does not bow-ride.

Dall's Porpoise

Phocoenoides dalli

To 7′3″ (2.2 m) long. Weight to 485 lb. (218 kg). Hooked, triangular dorsal fin, often with white patch. Thick body, grey to black with white patch on sides and belly. Common and abundant. Fast swimmer; creates "rooster tail" splash.

Pacific White-Sided Dolphin
Lagenorhynchus obliquedens
To 8′ (2.4 m) long. Weight to 300 lb. (135 kg). Tall, curved dorsal fin, black and grey. Black back with pale grey streak along sides, widening at tail end. Most abundant dolphin in north Pacific. Fast swimmer, leaps and creates "rooster tail" splash. In groups of 50 to several hundred.

Orca (Killer Whale)
Orcinus orca
Female to 23′ (7 m), 4.5 tons (4 tonnes), short curved dorsal fin to 3′ (90 cm). Male larger, to 30′ (9 m) and 6 tons (5.4 tonnes), tall dorsal fin to 6′ (1.8 m). Black with white chin, white patches behind eye and on sides. Dorsal fins and distinctive saddle patches behind dorsal fin used for identification. Family groups have unique vocalizations. Nearshore pods (5–50 animals) of resident orcas feed only on fish. Small pods (2–10 animals) of transient orcas are mammal hunters. Offshore orcas (pods to 25 or more animals) are likely fish eaters, especially sharks.

Gray Whale ▼
Eschrichtius robustus
To 50′ (15 m) long. Weight to 35 tons (31.5 tonnes). Long, slender head. A baleen whale (feeds by straining food through baleen plates in the jaws). Upper jaw has coarse yellow baleen. Grey body with lighter patches and mottling, scattered patches of white barnacles and orange whale lice. Low dorsal "hump," followed by 6 to 12 "knuckles." Marks on body sides and tail flukes are used to identify individuals. In shallow coastal waters; whales breed in shallow lagoons of Baja and migrate annually to Arctic seas.

Humpback Whale
Megaptera novaengliae
To 49'3"(14.8 m) long. Weight to 44 tons (40 tonnes). Large head with small knobs. A baleen whale. Low, stubby dorsal fin with broad base. Long, slender, lumpy flippers. Grey to black body with lighter underside. Alone or in groups of 20 or more. Swims actively, breaching, spy-hopping and rolling on back to wave flippers. Many feeding behaviours, lunging and bubble-netting. Colour and shape of underside of tail flukes are used to identify individuals.

Seals, Sea Lions

Pacific Harbour Seal
Phoca vitulina richardsi
Male and female to 6' (1.8 m) long. Weight to 250 lb. (113 kg). Large, round, smooth head without external ear flaps. Short, furry front flippers. Grey to black, mottled. Often hauls out on rocks and sand or mudflats.

Steller Sea Lion
Eumetopias jubatus
Female to 8' (2.4 m), 600 lb. (270 kg); male to 10' (3 m), 2,200 lb. (990 kg). Ear flaps; low forehead. Large front flippers to sit erect. Male tan above and reddish brown below; female slimmer and uniformly brown. Roars and growls, does not bark. Hauls out on rocks.

California Sea Lion

Zalophus californianus

Female to 5'8" (1.7 m), 250 lb. (113 kg); male to 8' (2.4 m) and 900 lb. (405 kg). Ear flaps. Smaller and darker than Steller sea lion. Mature male dark brown to tan, light-coloured bump on forehead. Female blonde to tan. Barks. Hauls out on rocks, logs and docks. Males and the occasional female migrate north of the breeding grounds in California and Mexico.

Sea Otter, River Otter

Sea Otter

Enhydra lutris

To 5' (1.5 m) long. Weight to 80 lb. (36 kg). Short, flattened tail. Short, thick neck and flat, broad head. Large, webbed hind feet. Tan or rusty red to dark brown or black, with light-coloured head. Squeals, hisses and grunts. Uses rock as a tool while eating and floating belly-up. Often swims on its back. Typically in open, exposed waters, solitary or "rafts" in kelp beds. Clumsy on land, seldom leaves the water.

River Otter ▼

Lutra canadiensis

To 4'6" (1.4 m) long. Weight to 30 lb. (13.5 kg). Long, round, tapered tail. Slender body and long neck, small, webbed hind feet. Short, dense dark fur above, lighter below. Unique whistle. Often swims belly-down. At home on land. Frequents marine waters.

Fishes
Phylum Chordata

Cartilaginous Fishes
These fishes, including sharks, rays and skates, have cartilaginous skeletons.

Spiny Dogfish
Squalus acanthias
To 5'3" (1.6 m) long. Weight to 20 lb. (9 kg). Long, slender shark. Slate grey to brown with grey-white underside. A single spine at the front of each of the top (dorsal) fins. Small mouth. Bears live young, rather than eggs. At surface to 2,400' (720 m).

Six Gill Shark
Hexanchus griseus
To 26'5" (8.8 m) long. Large head, 6 gill slits and a single dorsal fin. Dark brown to slate-grey with pale underside. Known as a "cow shark," not known to be aggressive toward divers. Usually in deep waters, has been seen regularly at 3,100' (933 m).

Ratfish
Hydrolagus colliei
To 39" (1 m) long. Large snout, small mouth with forward-pointing teeth. Long, tapering tail. Grey-brown body with white spots and silver underside. Swims by flapping forward fins. Male has large claspers on underside. Female lays eggs in elongated cases. Often in shallows, 30–3,085' (9–925 m) deep.

Big Skate
Raja binoculata
To 8' (2.4 m) long overall. Weight 200 lb. (90 kg)+. Pointed, V-shaped snout. Large eye-like spots near centre of each pectoral fin. Brown to dark grey. Rests on bottom, often partially buried, 10–2,625' (3–788 m) deep.

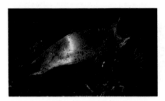

Skate Egg Cases (Mermaid's Purse)

Egg case of each species has a unique shape. Case of the big skate, *Raja binoculata*, may be up to 12" (30 cm) long and contain as many as 7 eggs. Often washed up on shore.

Bony Fishes

These fishes (p 15-20) have bony skeletons and a variety of body shapes. Many are the familiar species seen in tidepools and on reefs.

Tidepool Sculpin

Oligocottus maculosus

To 3½" (9 cm) long. Slender body, single forked spine on gill cover. Colour varies, often red-brown to green; 5 irregular dark saddles across the back. Common only in tidepools.

Scaleyhead Sculpin

Artedius harringtoni

To 4" (10 cm) long. 2 pairs of bush appendages on head of male. Colour varies from red to brown; white spot at base of caudal fin. At 16–35' (5–10.5 m) deep.

Longfin Sculpin

Jordania zonope

To 6" (15 cm) long. Slender, tapered body. Colourful olive green, red-orange and blue bands. Distinctive pale bands on head. At 6–60' (2–15 m) deep.

Sailfin Sculpin

Nautichthys oculofasciatus

To 8" (20 cm) long. Pink-orange to brown with bands on the back. Unique tall, sail-like first dorsal fin. In crevices, on pilings in shallow subtidal to 360' (108 m) deep.

Red Irish Lord ▼

Hemilepidotus hemilepidotus
To 20" (50 cm) long. Large head and eyes, conspicuous band of scales 4 to 5 wide, along sides. Colourful yet camouflaged, with red patches and brown, black and white mottling. In rocky areas, usually motionless, intertidal to 162' (49 m) deep.

Buffalo Sculpin

Enophrys bison
To 14½" (36 cm) long. Large head with pair of prominent spines on gill cover. Raised plates along high lateral line. Colour varies from brown to pink and green, with 4 dark saddles across the back. Pink egg mass. On rocky reefs, 3–60' (1–15 m) deep.

Cabezon

Scorpaenichthys marmoratus
To 39" (1 m) long. Weight to 30 lb. (13.5 kg). Large head, tapered body. Bushy, flap-like appendage on snout and above each eye. Marbled olive green to brown or grey, well camouflaged. On rocky reefs, in kelp, intertidal to 250' (75 m) deep.

Grunt Sculpin

Rhamphocottus richardsoni
To 3¼" (8 cm) long. Unique short, stout body with pointed snout and small eye. Tan to orange with dark bands. "Hops" along the bottom. In empty barnacle shells, in sponges or rocky crevices, 6–540' (2–165 m) deep.

Rockfishes

Many of these common and popular commercial and sport fishes are long-lived, but reef populations are easily overfished. Many Rockfish Conservation Areas (RCAs) have been established with fishery closures.

Quillback Rockfish
Sebastes maliger
To 2' (60 cm) long. Dark brown to black, mottled with yellow and orange. High, spiny dorsal fin with yellow streak in forward region. On rocky reefs, surface to 480' (144 m) deep.

Copper Rockfish
Sebastes caurinus
To 22" (55 cm) long. Olive-brown to copper with yellow and white blotches. Dark bands radiate from the eye. On rocky reefs, 30–600' (9–180 m) deep.

Yelloweye Rockfish
Sebastes ruberrimus
To 3' (90 cm) long. Orange-red to red-yellow body. Adults (A) have brilliant yellow eye on rough head. Juveniles (B) have dark eyes and 2 white bands along the sides that fade in time. Individuals are long-term residents at specific sites, 60–1,800' (18–540 m) deep.

China Rockfish
Sebastes nebulosus
To 17" (42.5 cm) long. Black body with broad yellow stripe and patches. Solitary species, resident on reefs, 13–422' (3.9–127 m) deep.

Tiger Rockfish ▼

Sebastes nigrocinctus

To 2' (60 cm) long. Pink to red with 5 vertical dark bands. Solitary and territorial, 3–900' (1–270 m) deep.

Black Rockfish

Sebastes melanops

To 25" (62.5 cm) long. Light to dark grey with dark mottling along upper back and a pale band below lateral line. In schools, often with other rockfish, surface to 1,200' (360 m) deep.

Yellowtail Rockfish

Sebastes flavidus

To 26" (65 cm) long. Olive green to green-brown with pale spots along back, yellow-green on fins. In schools, surface to 1,800' (540 m) deep.

Canary Rockfish

Sebastes pinniger

To 30" (75 cm) long. Orange body (A) with white to grey stripe along lateral line, 3 bright stripes across head. Juvenile (B) has a prominent dark spot at rear of spiny dorsal fin. In schools, rocky reefs, 60–1,200' (18–360 m) deep.

Lingcod, Greenlings

Lingcod
Ophiodon elongatus
To 5' (1.5 m) long. Weight to 105 lb. (47 kg). Large head, mouth and teeth. Long, tapered body with dark blotches, mottled grey, brown or green. Male guards egg masses in shallows. In kelp beds and on rocky reefs to 6,600' (1,980 m) deep.

Kelp Greenling ▼
Hexagrammos decagrammos
To 2' (60 cm) long. Male (A) brown-olive with bright blue spots, female (B) light brown, golden to blue, with rows of round orange-brown spots. Small, bushy appendage above each eye. Male guards pale blue to mauve egg mass. In kelp beds and rocky areas, intertidal to 150' (45 m) deep.

Painted Greenling
Oxylebius pictus
To 10" (25 cm) long. Long, pointed head with 2 pairs of bushy appendages. Dark vertical bars cross body and dorsal fin. Male guards orange egg mass. Sometimes associate with white-spotted anemone (p. 72). On rocky reefs to 162' (49 m) deep.

Perches

Shiner Perch
Cymatogaster aggregata
To 6" (15 cm) long. Small, silvery oval body, compressed, with large scales. Strong dark bars along sides, interrupted by 3 yellow vertical bars. In schools around pilings and floats and in kelp beds, surface to 480' (144 m) deep.

Striped Perch
Embiotica lateralis
To 15" (37.5 cm) long. Copper-coloured with about 15 iridescent blue horizontal stripes below lateral line. Common, solitary or in schools, near surface to 70' (21 m) deep.

Pile Perch
Rhacochilus vacca
To 17" (42.5 cm) long. Silvery, usually with dark, indistinct vertical bars. Black spot behind mouth. Deeply forked tail fin. Around floats, pilings and reefs, surface to 260' (78 m) deep.

Other Common Bony Fishes

Black-Eye Gobey
Rhinogobiops nicholsi
To 6" (15 cm) long. Black eyes, black patch at top of forward dorsal fin. Pale to dark tan-orange body with large scales. Territorial, in rock rubble, intertidal to 340' (102 m) deep.

Northern Ronquil
Ronquilis jordani
To 7" (17.5 cm) long. Elongated body with orange bands or spots below the eyes. Orange-cream to brown, olive green and grey. Long, single dorsal fin. In rock rubble, 10–540' (3–162 m) deep.

Northern Clingfish
Gobiesox maeandricus
To 6" (15 cm) long. Large head and flattened body; adhesive disc on underside. Dark, net-like pattern over body, often with pale band between and below eyes. On undersides of rocks, intertidal to 30' (9 m) deep.

Plainfin Midshipman

Porichthys notatus

To 15" (37.5 cm) long. Large mouth and head, tapered body (A). Dark grey-brown to purple with rows of luminous white spots. Female deposits and male guards yellow-orange clusters of eggs (B) under intertidal rocks. On sand–mud, intertidal to 1,200' (360 m). At low tide, males are sometimes heard "humming" a low song. Important prey for eagles, herons, seagulls and crows.

Warbonnets, Wolf Eels, Gunnels

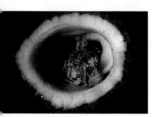

Decorated Warbonnet

Chirolophis decoratus

To 16½" (41 cm) long. Long head with large, bushy appendages centred in front of eyes to back of head. Long body, orange to brown with dark mottling and bars on fins. In crevices and sponges, 5–300' (1.5–90 m) deep.

Mosshead Warbonnet ▼

Chirolophis nugator

To 6" (15 cm) long. Numerous short, bushy appendages on head. Evenly spaced "eye spots" or bars along dorsal fin. In holes, crevices and empty barnacle shells, intertidal to 200' (60 m) deep.

Crescent Gunnel

Pholis laeta

To 10" (25 cm) long. Long and eel-like. Lime-green with crescent-shaped markings along the back. Under rocks and seaweeds, intertidal to 240' (72 m) deep.

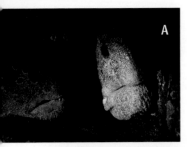

Wolf-Eel ▼
Anarrichthys ocellatus
To 8′ (2.4 m) long. Large head and mouth. Long, tapering body with black "eye spots." Female with dark, rounded head (A, left) and male with lighter bulbous head (A, right) often pair for life and guard eggs in den. Juveniles bright orange. Intertidal to 700′ (210 m) deep.

Flatfish (Flounders)

CO-Sole
Pleuronicthys coenosus
To 14″ (35 cm) long. Oval body with high sides. Large, dark spot on centre of back resembles the letters CO. Large, prominent eyes. On sand and in eelgrass beds, shallows to 1,200′ (360 m) deep.

Rock Sole
Pleuronectes bilineatus
To 2′ (60 cm) long. Black and yellow patches on fins, yellow spots along margins of side. Prominent arch in lateral line. Often rests on fins, unlike most other flounders. In sand or mud, intertidal to 1,500′ (450 m) deep.

English Sole
Pleuronectes vetulus
To 22½″ (56 cm) long. Pointed head, large eyes. Slender body, lateral line without high arch. Variable colour patterns. Often partially buried in sand or mud, intertidal to 1,800′ (540 m) deep.

Nudibranchs (Sea Slugs)
Phylum *Mollusca*

Nudibranchs are colourful—sometimes spectacular—favourites of tidepool explorers and divers. Many species have a retractable plume-like gill projection or numerous cerata (protrusions), shaped like fingers, paddles or clubs. Some also have papillae (finger-like projections) or tubercles (bumps) on the body for respiration, camouflage and defence.

Dorid Nudibranchs

Features include flattened body, retractable gill plume and rhinophores (paired sensory organs on the head). Dorids lay lacy ribbons of eggs.

Spotted Leopard Dorid
Diaulula odonoghuei

To 3" (7.5 cm) long. Elongated oval body with fine tubercles (bumps). Dark brown spots, solid or occasionally ring-shaped, that extend onto the mantle margin. On rocks and sponges, intertidal to 115' (35 m) deep. Ringed Leopard Dorid, *D. sandiegensis,* is more humped and has only a few dark rings or spots on body, found on open coast.

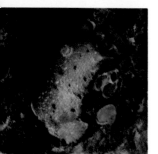

Monterey Sea Lemon
Doris montereyensis

To 6" (15 cm) long. Slender. Yellow to orange; scattered dark tubercles (bumps). Gills yellow colour. Feeds on sponges. Usually intertidal, but subtidal to 165' (50 m) deep. More common intertidally in protected waters. The Noble Sea Lemon, *Peltodoris nobilis*, has dark spots between the tubercles.

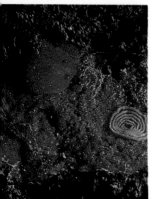

Red Nudibranch
Rostanga pulchra

To 5/8" (1.5 cm) long. Oval. Red-orange, sometimes with brown to black spots. Lays red ribbons of eggs and feeds on the velvety red sponge (p. 77). Intertidal and shallow subtidal, to 65' (20 m).

Clown Dorid
Triopha modesta
To 6" (15 cm) long. Slender body. White with orange on rhinophores (paired sensory organs on the head), front veil, branching tubercles (bumps) and gill plume. Feeds on spiral bryozoans (p. 83). Intertidal to 115' (35 m) deep. *T. catalinae* has knobby red tubercles, redder gill plume.

Noble Sea Lemon
Doris nobilis
To 8" (20 cm) long. Yellow to orange; dark spots between tubercles (bumps). Plume gills with white tips. Feeds on sponges. Intertidal on the open coast, usually subtidal to 750' (225 m) deep.

Giant White Dorid
Doris odhneri
To 8" (20 cm) long. Large bright white body with many large, wide-spaced tubercles. On rocks and sponges, intertidal to 75' (22.5 m) deep.

Barnacle Nudibranch
Onchidoris bilamellata
To ¾" (2 cm) long. Oval. Cream-coloured with or without pale to dark brown patterns on rough back. They are often found laying white ribbons of eggs. Feeds on barnacles. Intertidal.

Redgilled (Nanaimo) Dorid
Acanthodoris nanaimoensis
To 2" (5 cm) long. Round. White to dark grey with long yellow-tipped papillae (finger-like projections); faint to dark maroon highlights on gill plume and rhinophores (paired sensory organs on the head). Intertidal and shallow subtidal to 55' (17 m).

Yellow Margin Dorid

Cadlina luteomarginata

To 3" (8 cm) long. Oval. White with yellow margin. Low tubercles (bumps), tipped with yellow. Intertidal to 150' (45 m) deep.

Hudson's Yellow Margin Nudibranch

Acanthodoris hudsoni

To 1½" (4 cm) long. Egg-shaped body. White with yellow margin, yellow papillae (finger-like projections). Long rhinophores (paired sensory organs on the head). Intertidal and shallow subtidal.

Dendronotid Nudibranchs

Features include highly branched cerata (appendages) or gill-tufts and sheathed rhinophores (paired sensory organs on the head). Dendronotids lay coiled strings of eggs.

Giant Dendronotid

Dendronotus iris

To 10" (25 cm) long. Long, branched protrusions on back, frontal veil of 4 paired appendages. Colour varies from white to grey, orange or red. White line along foot margin. Common; feeds on tube-dwelling anemone (p. 73). Shallow subtidal 55' (17 m) or more.

Giant Red Dendronotid ▼

Dendronotus rufus

To 11" (27.5 cm) long. Long body. White, often with red-maroon spots. All appendages have red-maroon tips. Red-maroon line along foot margin. On rocks and algae, shallow subtidal.

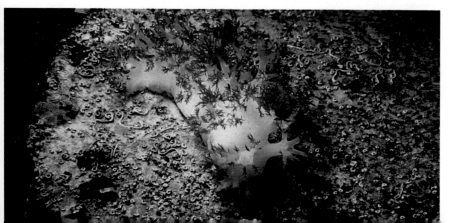

Variable Dendronotid
Dendronotus albus
To 2" (5 cm) long. Slender body. White to lilac. Top third of gill tufts and cerata (appendages) white, orange or both. White stripe down tail from behind last pair of gill tufts. On rocks and hydroids, shallow subtidal.

Dall's Dendronotid
Dendronotus dalli
To 5½" (14 cm) long. Long white body with branched, white-tipped appendages. Feeds on hydroids (pp. 74–75). On rocks, shallow subtidal subtidal, to 70' (21 m).

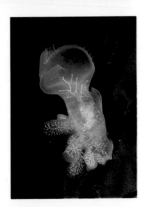

Hooded Nudibranch
Melibe leonina
To 4" (10 cm) long. Slender body. Translucent white, yellow-brown to green-brown and spotted. Has paddle-like appendages and a large hood with 2 fringes of tentacles to capture prey. On rocks and kelp, intertidal and shallow subtidal.

Orange Peel Nudibranch
Tochuina gigantea
To 12" (30 cm) long. Long body. Brilliant yellow-orange with white tubercles (bumps) and white tufts along edges. Feeds on hydroids (pp. 74–75), sea pens (p. 68) and soft corals (p. 69). Shallow subtidal.

Pink Tritonia
Tritonia exsulans
To 11¾" (30 cm) long. Broad oval body with gill tufts around edge. White line along margin of foot. Feeds on white and orange sea pens (p. 68). On sand–mud, shallow subtidal.

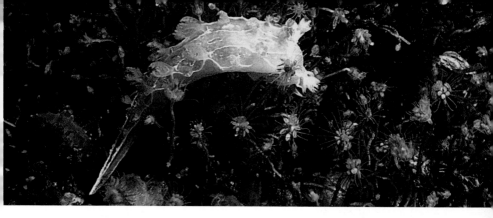

Diamond Back Tritonia ▲
Tritonia festiva
To 4" (10 cm) long. Slender body with tufts around edge. White to pink, usually with white diamond pattern on the back. Often feeds on soft corals (p. 69). Low intertidal to 165' (50 m) deep.

Arminacea Nudibranchs
Features include numerous groups or rows of cerata (appendages) or gill-tufts, frontal veil and unsheathed rhinophores (paired sensory organs on the head). They lay coiled strings of eggs.

Striped Nudibranch
Armina californica
To 2¾" (7 cm) long. Smooth brown body with raised longitudinal ridges. No visible cerata (appendages) at edges. Often feeds on orange sea pens (at right in photo). In sand–mud, shallow subtidal to 755' (226 m) deep.

White-Lined Dirona
Dirona albolineata
To 7" (17.5 cm) long. Translucent body with wide front veil. Grey or white to purple with large, flattened, pointed, white-edged appendages. On rocks, intertidal to 115' (35 m) deep.

Gold Dirona
Dirona pelucida
To 5" (12.5 cm) long. Oval body. Orange with white spots, lines and on tips of bulbous cerata (appendages). Feeds on bryozoans (pp. 83–84). On rocks, kelp and mud, shallow subtidal to 80' (24 m).

Aeolid Nudibranchs

Features include long oral tentacles, groups or rows of cerata (appendages) on the back, and long, fleshy rhinophores (paired sensory organs on the head).

Opalescent Nudibranch

Hermissenda crassicornis

To 2" (5 cm) long. Slender body, numerous cerata (appendages) with white lines, each topped with orange band and white tip. Often has orange areas on back, bordered by blue. Common on rocks and floats, intertidal to 115' (35 m) deep. This species is found from Alaska to northern California.

Shaggy Mouse Nudibranch

Aeolidia loui

To 2³/₈" (6 cm) long. Bare back, numerous shaggy appendages crowded along margins. Rough or warty (upright) rhinophores. White to grey-brown, usually with a large, triangular patch at front of head region. On rocks or mudflats, intertidal to 2,500' (750 m) deep.

Pearly Nudibranch

Ziminella japonica

To 3" (7.5 cm) long. Pearly cream to pink body, bare back with dense cerata (appendages) along margins. On rocks, shallow subtidal, to 65' (20 m).

Threelined Nudibranch

Orienthella trilineata

To 1³/₈" (3.4 cm) long. Slender white body with three white lines down back. Light red to orange appendages in clusters along margins. White rings on the rhinophores (paired sensory organs on the head). Feeds on hydroids. Low intertidal to 65' (20 m) deep.

Red Warty Nudibranch
Coryphella verrucosa
To 4" (10 cm) long. Slender, translucent white body with short, rounded head. Clusters of brick red cerata with white tips along the margins. Shallow subtidal, to 66' (20 m).

Long-mouth Red Himatima ▼
Himatima trophina
To 4" (10 cm) long. Slender, translucent white body with long, pointed head. Red-pink appendages with white tips along margins. Faint bars on rhinophores (paired sensory organs on the head). On rocks, mud or hydroids (pp. 74–75), low intertidal to at least 65' (20 m).

Spanish Shawl ▼
Flabellina iodinea
To 1½" (3.8 cm) long. Deep purple body with orange-tipped cerata (appendages). Feeds on hydroids. On rocky exposed coasts, intertidal to 120' (36 m) deep.

Octopus & Squid
Phylum Mollusca

Giant Pacific Octopus ▼
Enteroctopus dofleini (=Octopus dofleini)
To 16' (5 m) long from top of head to ends of arms. 8 arms of equal length, each 3 to 5 times body length. Skin wrinkled and folded. Animal (A) changes colour from pale to dark reddish brown, sometimes mottled. White streak in skin running through each eye, and single white spot in skin in front of eyes. Female guards clusters of eggs the size of rice grains (B) attached to roof of den. Intertidal to 1,650' (495 m) deep.

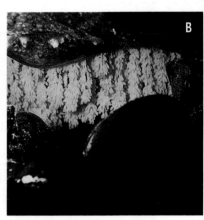

Red Octopus ▼
Octopus rubescens
To 20" (50 cm) long from top of head to ends of arms, mantle to 4" (10 cm) long. Each arm is 4 times body length. Can be distinguished from giant octopus (above) by 3 papillae (finger-like projections) under each eye and 2 white spots in skin at front of eyes. Octopus (A) found in bottles or empty shells (B), which serve as dens, in sandy and rocky areas, intertidal to 660' (200 m) deep.

Stubby Squid ▼
Rossia pacifica

To 3" (7.5 cm) long from top of head to ends of arms, mantle to 1½" (3.8 cm) long. Body (A) has small semicircular fins. Reddish brown with pale underside. Has 2 long tentacles, kept in a sheath and deployed to capture prey. Clusters of round eggs with points on ends opposite attachment (B) are laid on rocks. On rocks or in sand–mud (buried in daytime, on surface at night), subtidal, 50–1,215' (15–365 m) deep.

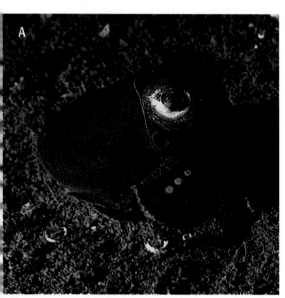

Opalescent Squid ▼
Doryteuthis (Amerigo) opalescens

To 11" (27.5 cm) long from top of head to ends of arms, cylindrical mantle to 8" (20 cm) long. 8 short arms, 2 long tentacles. Animal (A) changes colour from translucent white to mottled brown and gold. Schools of squid mate in shallow sandy bays and lay clusters of finger-like eggs (B). In coastal shallows and offshore surface waters to bottom.

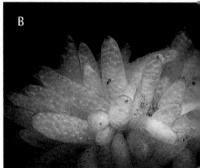

Bivalves & Lampshells
Clams, Mussels, Oysters, Scallops, Cockles & Lampshells
Phylum Mollusca, Phylum Brachiopoda

Bivalves ("two shells") are a class of molluscs, a large, diverse group of animals with soft, unsegmented bodies. The lampshell, while very similar in appearance, is a brachiopod ("arm foot"), a very different animal.

Mussels

Mussel shells are symmetrical, elongated and typically attached in clumps by strong, thin byssus (thread-like secretion). Mussels are common and abundant on floating structures, pilings, and intertidal and subtidal rocks and gravel. There is likely one native species of blue mussel, the most common species in the region—Pacific blue mussel (*Mytilus trossulus*)—and several distinct introduced species of bay and blue mussels. These species are difficult to identify by their shells alone and the situation is complicated by the existence of many hybrids.

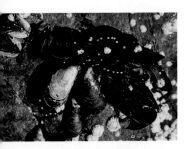

Pacific Blue Mussel
Mytilus trossulus
To 4½" (11 cm) long. Elongated, narrow, curved anterior end. Bluish black, often with purplish eroded area. Native species; on floating structures, pilings, rocks and gravel, intertidal and subtidal.

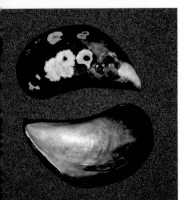

Mediterranean Blue (Gallo's) Mussel
Mytilus galloprovincialis
To 6" (15 cm) long. Broad, triangular fan-shaped black shell, pointed anterior end. Introduced from the Atlantic for aquaculture. On floating structures, pilings, rocks and gravel, intertidal and subtidal.

Blue Mussel
Mytilus edulis

To 4½" (11 cm) long. Elongated, narrow end. Ventral margin straight or somewhat curved. Introduced from the Atlantic for aquaculture. On floating structures, pilings, rocks and gravel, intertidal and subtidal.

California Mussel
Mytilus californianus

To 10" (25 cm) long. Thick shells, pointed at anterior end. Strong ribs run along length of shell, often worn off on larger specimens. Exterior may have tan radial rays. Bright orange meat. On exposed oceanic coasts, intertidal to 330' (100 m) deep.

Northern Horsemussel
Modiolus modiolus

To 7" (17.5 cm) long. Oval, inflated, length is usually twice the height and width. Purple shell covered with brown, hairy periostracum (thin covering). Often in aggregations in gravel, intertidal to 660' (200 m) deep.

Oysters

The lower shell of the oyster is usually cupped and often attached; the upper shell is flattened and smaller than the lower. The height of oyster shells is measured from the hinge to the outer margin. Only one species of oyster, Olympia oyster (below), is native to this coast. Three other species have been introduced for aquaculture and some have spawned to seed other beaches. The most common and abundant of these is the Pacific Japanese oyster.

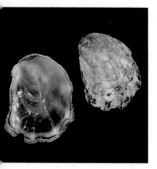

Olympia Oyster
Ostrea lurida

To 3½" (9 cm) diameter. Round to oval shell, often frilled and fluted. Exterior grey, purple or white. Interior greenish to purple with dark muscle scar. Small bumps (chomata) along interior margin, near hinge. On rocks, intertidal to 33' (10 m).

Pacific Japanese Oyster
Crassostrea gigas
To 12" (30 cm) high. Shell often fluted. Exterior grey-white with purple-black new growth. Interior smooth, white with light-coloured muscle scar. Introduced from Japan. On firm substrates, intertidal.

European Flat Oyster
Ostrea edulis
To 3" (7.5 cm) high. Round to pear-shaped with ribs and frilly growth margins. Exterior varies from white to yellow, tan and purple. Interior white. Introduced from Europe. On firm substrates, intertidal.

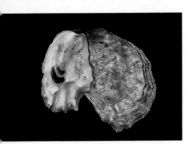

Atlantic Oyster
Crassostrea virginica
To 8" (20 cm) high. Irregular outline. Thick, elongated, ridged shell. Tan to purple, sometimes with ray pattern. Interior white with purple muscle scar. Introduced from the western Atlantic. On firm substrates, intertidal.

Scallops
Scallops have unequal shells with strong radial ribs and wing-like hinges ("ears"). Eyes around the edge of the mantle are visible between the gaping shells. A scallop may be free-swimming, or attached to a hard surface. Some are heavily encrusted with sponges. There are small fisheries for swimming scallops (mostly the spiny pink) by divers and small trawls.

Rock Scallop
Crassadoma gigantea
To 10" (25 cm) high. Thick, round, ribbed shells, often infested with yellow boring sponge (p. 77). Orange mantle with blue eyes. White interior; purple-stained hinge. Cemented to rocks, intertidal to 260' (78 m) deep.

Spiny Pink Scallop
Chlamys hastata
To 3¼" (8 cm) high. Almost round pink shells with fluted margin. Wide, coarse primary ribs with strong spines and several riblets between. On rocky reefs, 7–495' (2–150 m) deep.

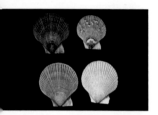

Smooth Pink Scallop
Chlamys rubida
To 2½" (6.3 cm) high. Round shells, prominent radial ribs without strong spines. Upper shell pink to red-purple, white or yellow. Lower shell paler. On mud–gravel, 3–665' (1–200 m) deep.

Japanese Scallop
Mizuhopecten yessoensis
To 9" (22.5 cm) high. Upper shell purple-grey with flattened ribs. Interior margin dark purple. Lower shell white and thick, with rounded ribs. Introduced from Japan to BC in 1980s for aquaculture.

Weathervane Scallop
Patinopecten caurinus
To 11" (27.5 cm) high (largest free-swimming scallop in the world). Round shells. Upper shell red-pink to grey with about 17 rounded ribs; lower shell nearly white with about 24 broad, flattened square ribs. In depressions in sand or gravel, 33–660' (10–200 m) deep; sometimes washed ashore.

Cockles

Nuttall's Heart Cockle
Clinocardium nuttallii
To 5½" (14 cm) long. 34–38 strong ribs, crossed by wavy lines at the margins. Yellow-brown; young mottled with red-brown. Buried near surface of sand, intertidal to 100' (30 m) deep.

Clams

Manila Clam
Venerupis philippinarum
To 3" (7.5 cm) long. Elongated oval shells, flattened, with lattice sculpture. Radial ribs are stronger. Colour varies from grey to brown, often streaked, occasionally with angular patterns (A). Shell interior often stained with yellow and purple (B). Inside edge of shell is smooth. Short siphons, split at tip. In sand–mud–gravel, high to mid-intertidal.

Littleneck Clam ▼
Leukoma staminea
To 3" (7.5 cm) long. Round to oval shells, inflated, with lattice sculpture. White to brown in colour, often with angular patterns. Interior white. Inside edge of shell has fine teeth. Short siphons, fused at tip. In sand–mud–gravel, mid- to low intertidal, to 35' (10 m) deep.

Butter Clam
Saxidomus gigantea
To 5¼" (13 cm) long. Oval to squarish shell with concentric ridges. White to grey; shells gape at posterior (siphon) end. In sand–mud–gravel, mid- to low intertidal, to 130' (39 m) deep.

Dark Mahogany Clam
Nuttallia obscurata
To 2¾" (7 cm) long. Thin, flat oval shells. Shiny brown periostracum (shell covering), worn white at hinge. Interior purple, white. Long, separate siphons. Introduced from Japan in 1980s. Buried in sand–mud, high to mid-intertidal.

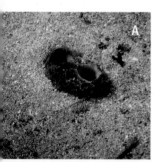

Razor Clam
Siliqua patula
To 7" (17.5 cm) long. Long, thin, narrow brittle shells. Rounded ends. Shiny, smooth periostracum (shell covering), olive to brown. Shell interior white with purple, slanting rib to anterior. On surf-exposed sandy beaches, intertidal to 180' (54 m).

Geoduck Clam ▼
Panopea abrupta
To 7¾" (19.5 cm) long. Weight to 10 lb. (4.5 kg) or more. Lives as long as 168 years! Shells are rounded at anterior end, truncated at siphon. Gaping at all sides, due to large body and neck. White shell, thin periostracum (shell covering) at margins. "Shows" (A) of long siphons from body (B) buried to 3' (90 cm) in sand–mud–shell–gravel, intertidal to 350' (105 m) deep.

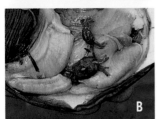

Fat Horse Clam

Tresus capax

To 7" (17.5 cm) long. Oval shell, length 1½ times the height, gaping at siphon. Hinged from a spoon-shaped socket. Siphons have leathery plates at the tip. Often hosts pea crabs (B). In sand–mud, intertidal to 100' (30 m) deep.

Pacific Horse Clam

Tresus nuttallii

To 9" (22.5 cm) long. Elongated shell, length more than 1½ times height. Weight to 3 lb. (1.4 kg). Hinged from a spoon-shaped socket. Rarely hosts pea crabs (see fat horse clam, above). Siphons have leathery plates at the tip. In sand–mud, intertidal to 165' (50 m) deep.

(Left) Flap-Tip Piddock

Penitella penita

To 3" (7.5 cm) long. Elongated shells, each with 3 sections and leathery pads at the end. Small siphon holes in soft rock, mud or clay, intertidal to 72' (22 m) deep.

(Right) Rough Piddock

Zirfaea pilsbryi

To 5¾" (14.4 cm) long. Large white shells with unique sculpture for burrowing. Shells are separated by groove and gape at both ends. Split siphons show at surface, body buried in limestone, shale and hard clay, intertidal to 412' (125 m) deep.

Softshell Clam
Mya arenaria
To 6" (15 cm) long. Elongated white shells with yellow or brown periostracum (thin covering), gaping at siphon end. Hinged from a spoon-shaped socket. Introduced from the Atlantic with oysters. In sand–mud, intertidal.

Northwest Ugly Clam ▼
Entodesma navicula
To 6" (15 cm) long. Elongated and variable shaped shell covered with red-brown periostracum (thin covering), which cracks when dried. In crevices, intertidal to 65' (20 m) deep.

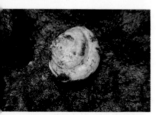

Baltic Macoma
Macoma balthica
To 1½" (3.8 cm) long. Oval shells, often pink, may be blue, orange or yellow. In sand–mud and eelgrass beds, intertidal to 130' (39 m) deep.

Bent-Nose Macoma
Macoma nasuta
To 3" (7.5 cm) long. Thin white shells bend to the right near the pointed posterior (siphon) end. In sand, intertidal to 165' (50 m) deep.

Green False-Jingle ▼
Pododesmus macrochisma
To 5¼" (13 cm) long. Thin, round shells. Lower shell has pear-shaped hole for a short, thick byssus (thread-like secretion) fixed with a calcareous attachment. On rocks, intertidal to 295' (88 m) deep.

Lampshells
Phylum Brachiopoda
The lampshell looks like a bivalve mollusc, but is a brachiopod with 2 shells and a soft body. It attaches to the bottom by a fleshy stalk that protrudes through the shell, and gathers food by sweeping the water with an arm-like structure.

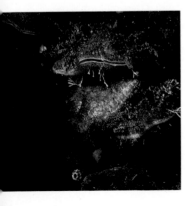

Lampshell
Terebratalia transversa
To 1¼" (3 cm) long. Smooth to prominently ribbed shells with tan to brown periostracum (thin covering). On rocks and rock faces, intertidal to 5,575' (1,672 m) deep.

Snails, Limpets & Abalone
Phylum Mollusca

Snails, limpets and abalone are single-shelled animals, all members of the gastropod ("belly foot") class. They are quite diverse in form.

Snails

Red Turban
Pomaulax gibberosus
To 3" (7.5 cm) high, 4½" (11 cm) diameter. Squat, reddish-brown, cone-shaped shell. Often covered with coralline algae (p. 92). Whorls have bumpy ridges. Base is flat and furrowed. Pearly operculum ("trap door"). Intertidal to 260' (78 m) deep.

Black Turban
Tegula funebralis
To 1¼" (3 cm) diameter. Thick black-purple shell, low cone with 4 whorls. Feeds on seaweeds. Common and abundant on rocks, intertidal. Often hosts a stack of Hooked slipper limpets, *Crepidula adunca*.

Purple-Ring Topsnail
Calliostoma annulatum
To 1¼" (3 cm) high. Conical shell with 8 to 9 whorls. Orange-yellow with bright purple-violet bands. On rocks along open coasts, intertidal to 100' (30 m) deep.

Blue Topsnail
Calliostoma ligatum
To 1" (2.5) diameter. Brown shell with light tan spiral ridges, worn patches show pearly blue inner layer. Rounded whorls and aperture. Rocky areas, intertidal to 100' (30 m) deep.

Spiny Topsnail
Cidarina cidaris
To 1½" (3.8 cm) high. Rounded, beaded whorls, longitudinal ridges. Exterior grey, whitish when worn. Interior pearly. Common on rocks, 50' (15 m) and deeper.

Hairy Oregon Triton
Fusitriton oregonensis
To 6" (15 cm) high. About 6 whorls with axial riblets, spiralling pairs of threads. Thick, shaggy, grey-brown periostracum (shell covering). On rocks, intertidal to 295' (88 m) deep.

Lewis' Moonsnail ▼
Neverita lewisii
To 5½" (14 cm) high. Large, globular shell, cream-coloured with thin brown periostracum (covering). Horny operculum ("trap door"), tan to brown, seals body in shell. Soft body (A) translucent brown, not blotched. Lays eggs in smooth, distinctive sand-covered egg collar (B). Drills and feeds on clams, leaving distinctive drill hole (C). In sand–mud, intertidal to 165' (50 m) deep.

Aleutian Moonsnail
Cryptonatica aleutica
To 2½" (6.3 cm) high. Shell cream to brown in colour. Calcareous operculum ("trap door"). Soft body, cream-coloured with rusty red to maroon blotches. In sand–mud, intertidal to 1,500' (450 m) deep.

Spindle (Dire) Whelk

Lirabuccinum dirum
To 2" (5 cm) high. Thick, strong shell. 9 to 11 low, rounded axial ribs. Numerous unsymmetrical spiral threads. Dull grey. On rocks, intertidal.

Leafy Hornmouth

Ceratostoma foliatum
To 3½" (9 cm) high. Large tooth projects from the aperture. White or white with brown bands; 3 wing-like projections or frills. Lays clusters of yellow egg capsules. Intertidal to 215' (65 m).

Northern Striped Dogwinkle

Nucella ostrina
To 1¼" (3 cm) high. Thick, plump shell, variable smooth to spiral cords, often banded. Exterior grey to black, brown or yellow. Interior of aperture often purple. Intertidal, feeds on mussels. Yellow egg capsules are short and vase-shaped.

Frilled Dogwinkle

Nucella lamellosa
To 3¼" (8 cm) high. Variable form, smooth (on exposed beaches) to wrinkled. Up to 12 axial frills. Banded shell, white to brown in colour. Lays clusters of stalked, pointed yellow egg capsules. Outer lip broadly flared with 3 rounded teeth. Intertidal to shallow subtidal.

Channeled Dogwinkle

Nucella canaliculata
To 1½" (3.8 cm) high. 14 to 16 slender spiral ridges, separated by deep furrows or secondary ridges (A). White to grey, orange, brown or pink. Feeds on barnacles and mussels. On rocks, intertidal. Eggs (B) with fine encircling ridges, two vertical ridges.

Mudflat Snail
Batillaria attramentaria
To 1¼" (3 cm) high. Small, elongated shell. 8 to 9 grey whorls with brown-beaded spiral ridges. Abundant on sand–mud, mid- to low intertidal.

Purple Olive ▼
Olivella biplicata
To 1¼" (3 cm) high. Long, smooth, shiny shell. Whitish to purple. Often leaves trail in the sand. On exposed sandy beaches, low intertidal to 150' (45 m) deep.

Limpets
The keyhole limpet can be identified by a hole near the apex (peak) of the shell. The "true" limpet has a single cone-shaped shell. Many limpets are preyed upon by sea stars, and show an escape response that may include twisting, releasing and falling, or "flight." Limpets graze on algae. They are often found in the shade or on the underside of rocks, intertidal and shallow subtidal.

Rough Keyhole Limpet
Diodora aspera
To 2¾" (7 cm) across. Oval shell with lattice sculpture. Apex (peak) slightly off-centre with circular opening at top. Scale worm (p. 81) may be found in underside groove. On rocks, low intertidal and shallow subtidal.

Whitecap Limpet

Acmaea mitra

To 1 3/8" (3.4 cm) diameter, 1¼" (3 cm) high. Thick round shell with central apex (peak). White or overgrown with coralline algae (p. 92), on which it feeds. On exposed coasts, intertidal and shallow subtidal.

Plate Limpet

Lottia scutum

To 1¾" (4.5 cm) diameter. Low, flattened shell with off-centre apex (peak). Green-grey with light and dark streaks or checkerboard pattern. Intertidal and shallow subtidal.

Mask Limpet

Lottia persona

To 2" (5 cm) diameter. Oval shell, smooth margin. Exterior blue-grey, brown and black at top, speckled with white. Interior blue-white with dark margin, often with white spots and a dark mask-like stain behind the apex (peak). On rocks, high intertidal.

Shield Limpet

Lottia pelta

To 1¾" (4.5 cm) diameter, 5/8" (1.5 cm) high. Oval shell, apex (peak) nearly at centre. Irregular ribbing. Exterior grey; irregular white radial stripes form a net pattern. Interior blue-white with brown spot. In mussel beds, often with sea palm (p. 91), sometimes on feather boa kelp (p. 91), intertidal.

Ribbed Limpet

Lottia digitalis

To 1¼" (3 cm) diameter. Elongated oval shell with apex (peak) near anterior. Prominent ribs radiate from apex. Exterior grey with olive-green bands. On exposed coasts, high intertidal and splash zones.

Abalone

Northern Abalone ▼
Haliotis kamtschatkana
To 7" (17.5 cm) long. Thin, elongated-oval shell with irregular surface and 3 to 6 open holes. Interior iridescent white. In kelp beds or on rocks, intertidal to 50' (15 m) deep.

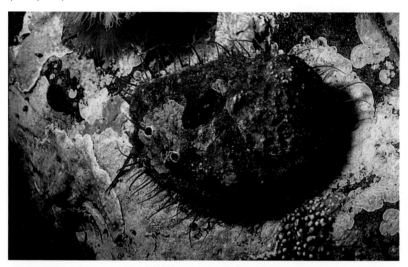

Chitons
Phylum Mollusca

These oval, flattened animals have 8 overlapping plates (valves) bound together with a leathery girdle. Most chitons live hidden under rocks, intertidal and shallow subtidal, and a few are common in tidepools.

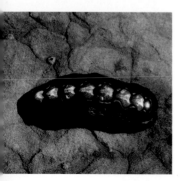

Leather Chiton
Katharina tunicata
To 3" (7.5 cm) long. Smooth girdle covering about 2/3 of the plates. Brown to black. On rocks in current and wave-swept areas, mid-intertidal.

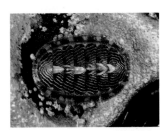

Lined Chiton
Tonicella lineata
To 2" (5 cm) long. Smooth, dark girdle, often banded. Red to orange-pink valves with dark zigzag lines edged with white. On rocks, grazing on coralline algae, pink rock crust (p. 92), 3–65' (1–20 m) deep.

Blue-Line Chiton
Tonicella undocaerulea
To 2" (5 cm) long. Smooth, banded girdle. Light orange to pink valves with concentric white zigzag lines, brilliant blue zigzag lines. On rocks, grazing on coralline algae, pink rock crust (p. 92), 3–165' (1–50 m) deep.

Mossy Chiton
Mopalia muscosa
To 2¾" (7 cm) long. Girdle has small notch in the rear, many stiff, stout hairs along edges. Valves dull, often worn, dark brown or grey to black. Valves may have growths of seaweed or barnacles. On rocks, intertidal.

Merten's Chiton
Lepidozona mertensii
To 1½" (3.8 cm) long. Girdle has low, smooth scales with yellow and reddish bands. Valves are reddish or green-purple, with strong white lines. On rocks, intertidal to 300' (90 m) deep.

Giant Pacific Chiton ▼
Cryptochiton stelleri
To 13" (32.5 cm) long. Body (A) has large plates, called butterfly shells (B), completely covered by brown to reddish brown girdle. Underside yellow with broad, edible foot. Intertidal to 65' (20 m) deep.

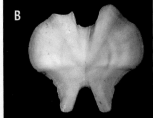

Crabs & Shrimp
Phylum Arthropoda

Crabs

Hairy Shore Crab
Hemigrapsus oregonensis
Carapace to 2" (5 cm) wide. Hairy legs, body grey to dark green, white or mottled. Under rocks, intertidal. Found in quiet bays, common on mud flats, sometimes in burrows.

Purple Shore Crab
Hemigrapsus nudus
Carapace to 2¼" (5.6 cm) wide. Square carapace, typically purple with dark spots on claws, but may be olive or red-brown. Walking legs smooth, not hairy. Under rocks and in crevices; high intertidal.

Black-Clawed Crab ▼
Lophopanopeus bellus bellus
Carapace to 1½" (3.8 cm) wide. Thick, smooth, heavy dark claws. Body colour varies from purple to grey to dark brown. Under rocks, intertidal.

Dungeness Crab ▼

Cancer magister

Carapace to 10" (25 cm) wide, widest at tenth and largest tooth. Carapace grey-brown and purple, legs grey-brown with orange, underside yellow. Male (A) has V-shaped abdomen, female has U-shaped abdomen. In sand–mud or eelgrass, intertidal to 750' (225 m) deep.

Slender Cancer Crab

Cancer gracilis

Carapace to 4½" (11 cm) wide. Broad marginal teeth outlined in white, legs purple, claws purple with white tips. Often mistaken for Dungeness crab. In sand–mud, intertidal to 470' (140 m).

Red Rock Crab ▼

Cancer productus

Carapace to 8" (20 cm) wide. Fan-shaped carapace is brick red (A). Claws have black-tipped pincers. Juvenile's colour variable (B), white to dark red streaked with white. In eelgrass, gravel and rocky areas, intertidal to 260' (78 m) deep.

Hairy Cancer Crab
Cancer oregonensis
Carapace to 2" (5 cm) wide. Dull red, circular carapace. Short, hairy legs. Claws have black-tipped pincers. In small holes and empty giant barnacle shells, low intertidal to 1,335′ (400 m) deep.

Slender Decorator Crab
Oregonia gracilis
Carapace to 1½" (3.8 cm) wide. Triangular carapace with 2 equally long horns. Long, slender walking legs. Grey or tan body, highly decorated with sponges, hydroids, algae and other organisms. On rocks, intertidal to 1,430′ (430 m) deep.

Northern Kelp Crab
Pugettia producta
Carapace to 3½" (9 cm) wide. Smooth carapace, red to olive in colour. Front margin straight or slightly curved between lateral teeth. Pointed legs. Underside yellow to scarlet. In kelp beds and on pilings, intertidal to 240′ (72 m) deep. Juveniles often on eelgrass.

Slender Kelp Crab
Pugettia gracilis
Carapace to 1 3/8" (3.4 cm) wide. Smooth carapace, brown, yellow or red. Front margin indented between teeth. Ends of claws are blue with red tips. On eelgrass, kelp and rocks, intertidal to 460′ (138 m) deep.

Sharp-Nose Crab
Scyra acutifrons
Carapace to 1¾" (4.4 cm) wide. 2 flattened, leaf-like horns. Short, stout walking legs and large, long claws. Rocky areas, low intertidal to 720' (215 m) deep.

Puget Sound King Crab ▼
Lopholithodes mandtii
Carapace to 12" (30 cm) wide. Box-like body with 4 large bumps on top. Colour is a mix of bright red, purple, orange. Juveniles are a uniform bright red. On rocky reefs in currents, shallow subtidal to 450' (135 m) deep.

Brown Box Crab
Lopholithodes foraminatus
Carapace to 8" (20 cm) wide. Boxy shape. Bumpy body, tan to red-brown. Unique circular holes between first walking legs and claws. In sand–mud, low intertidal to 1,800' (550 m) deep.

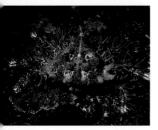

Heart Lithode
Phyllolithodes papillosus
Carapace to 3½" (9 cm) wide. Triangular carapace with raised heart-shaped outline. Body grey to brown with orange markings. Legs have long, flattened spines and white "socks." Rocky reefs, shallow subtidal to 600' (180 m) deep.

Hairy Lithode
Hapalogaster mertensii
Carapace to 1½" (3.8 cm) wide. Flattened, hairy brown body with flat, soft abdomen. Often under rocks in currents, intertidal to 180' (54 m) deep.

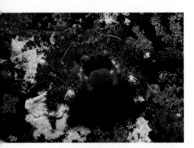

Golf-Ball Lithode
Rhinolithodes wosnessenskii
Carapace to 2½" (6.3 cm) wide. Triangular carapace with semicircular depression that forms a ball shape. Grey body with orange and white markings. On rock walls, subtidal 20–240' (6–72 m) deep.

Granular Claw Crab
Oedignathus inermis
Carapace to 1½" (3.8 cm) wide. Pear-shaped carapace with flattened abdomen. Large right claw with blue granules. In crevices and empty giant barnacle shells, intertidal to 60' (18 m) deep.

Red Fur Crab
Acantholithodes hispidus
Carapace to 2½" (6.3 cm) wide. Soft, spiny, hairy body dappled with red, brown and white. Claws bright red-orange. In sand–mud and rocky areas, intertidal to 540' (162 m) deep.

Flaring Turtle Crab
Cryptolithodes sitchensis
Carapace to 4" (10 cm) wide. Oval carapace covers legs and smooth claws. Rostrum (horn) flares at tip. Colours and patterns variable with orange, red and grey. On rocks, low intertidal to 60' (18 m) deep.

Butterfly Crab
Cryptolithodes typicus
Carapace to 3" (7.5 cm) wide. Oval carapace covers legs and smooth claws (A). Rostrum (horn) narrows at tip (B). White and black with patterns and shades of grey, pink and brown. On rocks, low intertidal to 150' (45 m) deep.

Squat Lobster
Munida quadrispina
Carapace to 3" (7.5 cm) long, body to 5" (12.5 cm) long. Lobster-like animal with long, slender claws. Red-brown to orange body. On or swimming above mud bottoms, subtidal 40–4,800' (135–1,440 m) deep.

Flat-top Porcelain Crab
Petrolisthes eriomerus
Carapace to ¾" (2 cm) wide. Flattened, dark brown body. Claws are broad and flat with bright blue markings. Drops legs when disturbed. Under rocks, intertidal to 280' (85 m) deep. *P. cinctipes* is found on or near the outer coast.

Thickclaw Porcelain Crab
Pachycheles rudis
Carapace to ¾" (2 cm) across, colour variable. Body with grey, brown and white markings. Large, unequal, rough claws with tubercles and scattered hairs. Intertidal and shallows, under rocks, in crevices and in kelp holdfasts.

Orange Hermit Crab
Elassochirus gilli
Carapace to 1½" (3.8 cm) long. Smooth, orange legs and claws, white spots at joints. Rocky areas, intertidal to 665' (200 m) deep.

Widehand Hermit Crab ▼

Elassochirus tenuimanus

Carapace to 1½" (3.8 cm) long. Large, flattened right claw with a wide "hand." Reddish brown to purple-blue on walking legs. On sand, mud, shell and gravel, intertidal to 1,275' (380 m) deep.

Hairy Hermit Crab

Pagurus hirsutiusculus

Small hermit crab with a body that grows to 7/10" (19 mm). The antennae are banded and there are white bands on the leg joints. The hermit crab's dark brown body is much larger than the tiny shell that is abandoned when in flight from predators. Very commonly found in tidepools.

Grainy Hand Hermit Crab

Pagurus granosimanus

Small intertidal hermit crab with a body to 4/5" (20 mm). It has distinctive orange antennae; body is dark olive green with pale blue–coloured granules. Commonly found in tidepools and can completely withdraw into the shell.

Bering Hermit Crab

Pagurus beringanus

Carapace to 1" (2.5 cm) long. Brown claws with red bumps and spines; pale blue walking legs with red bands and spots. Often found in large, heavy shell. In rocky areas, intertidal to 1,195' (358 m).

Shrimp

Broken Back Shrimp
Heptacarpus kincaidi
Carapace to ¼" (6 mm) long, body to 1 3/8" (3.4 cm) long. Prominent hump on back. Transparent body with red and yellow bars; white midrib on rostrum (horn). On rocks, at base of snakelock or painted anemone (p. 73), subtidal 33–600' (10–180 m) deep.

Candystripe Shrimp
Lebbeus grandimanus
Carapace to 3/8" (9 mm) long, body to 1 3/8" (3.4 cm) long. Transparent body with brilliant bands of red, yellow and blue. At base of snakelock, painted (p. 73), and other anemones, subtidal 20–590' (6–177 m) deep.

Coonstripe (Dock) Shrimp
Pandalus danae
Carapace to 1¼" (3 cm) long, body to 5½" (14 cm) long. Translucent body with red-brown irregular stripes, thin white lines and many fine blue spots. On pilings or rocks and in kelp, intertidal to 605' (181 m) deep.

Spot Prawn ▼
Pandalus platyceros
Carapace to 2 3/8" (6 cm) long, body to 10" (25 cm) long (females largest). Red body with conspicuous white spots, paired on the first and fifth abdominal sections. Carapace in head region has white bars. Rocky areas, intertidal to 1,600' (480 m) deep. Harvested in trap fisheries.

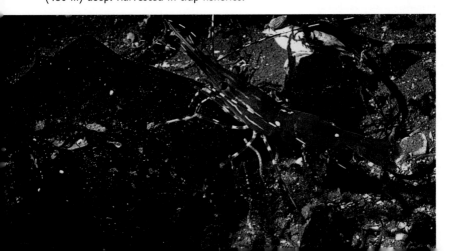

Spiny Pink Shrimp ▼
Pandalus eous
Carapace to 1" (2.5 cm) long, body to 5" (12.5 cm) long. Fine red dots over translucent body; spines along back and at posterior of third and fourth body segments. Soft sand–mud, subtidal 55–4,535′ (16.5–1,360 m) deep.

Blue Mud Shrimp
Upogebia pugettensis
To 6" (15 cm) long, ½" (1 cm) high. Speckled, tan-grey to blue-grey. Hairy legs; fan-shaped tail. First pair of legs unequal in size, with small claws. Burrows in sand–mud or mud–gravel, intertidal.

Ghost Shrimp
Neotrypaea californiensis
To 4 5/8" (11.5 cm) long, ¾" (2 cm) high. Smooth, slender body, pink, orange and yellow in colour. White, hairless claws are unequal in size. Male has huge claw. Makes U-shaped burrow; leaves volcano-like mound at entrance. In sand–mud, intertidal.

Small Crustaceans
Barnacles, Isopods & Amphipods
Phylum Arthropoda

Barnacles

Acorn Barnacle
Balanus glandula
To ¾" (2 cm) high, ¾" (2 cm) diameter. Small, white volcano-like shells and plates. Common on rocks, floats and pilings, intertidal.

Brown Barnacle
Chthamalus dalli
To ¼" (6 mm) diameter, 1/8" (3 mm) high. Grey-brown shell; brown cover plates form a cross. Highest barnacle in the intertidal.

Thatched Barnacle ▼
Semibalanus cariosus
To 2 3/8" (6 cm) diameter, 2½" (6.3 cm) high. Ribbed wall, "thatched" with downward pointing projections. White to dirty grey. Sometimes tall and crowded. On rocks, intertidal and subtidal to 180' (54 m) deep.

Goose Barnacle ▼
Pollicipes polymerus
To 1 1/8" (2.8 cm) wide at the crown, stalk to 6" (15 cm) high. Grows in clumps. Individual is a leathery stalk topped with 5 large plates and numerous small plates. On rocks, intertidal to 100' (30 m) deep.

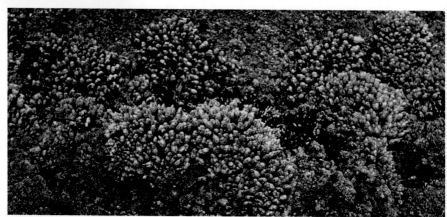

Giant Barnacle
Balanus nubilus
To 4" (10 cm) diameter, 5" (12.5 cm) high. Often in large clumps, 12" (30 cm) or more diameter. 2 of the 4 closing plates are hooked. On rocks, intertidal to 300' (90 m) deep.

Pelagic Goose Barnacle
Lepas anatifera
To 2¾" (7 cm) wide at crown, 8" (20 cm) long. Purple-brown on fleshy stalk. White plates with fine striations and orange along edges. On floating objects and on floating structures at surface.

Crenate Barnacle
Balanus crenatus
To 1" (2.5 cm) diameter. Squat, smooth and white. Base is crenulated. Grows on hard, smooth surfaces, including seaweeds. Low intertidal to 600' (182 m).

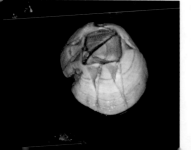

Kelp Isopod ▼
Idotea wosnesenskii
To 1 3/8" (3.4 cm) long. Elongated, flattened segmented body with thick antennae, 7 pairs of walking legs and a rounded tail section. Black, tan, pink-red and green. In mussels and on kelp and coralline algae (pink specimens), mid-intertidal to 50' (15 m) deep.

Beach Hopper (Amphipod)
Traskorchestia traskiana
To ¾" (2 cm) long. Dark grey body, transparent antennae. In seaweed drift, gravel, rocky and sand beaches, high intertidal.

Skeleton Shrimp (Caprellid Amphipod)
Caprella sp.
To 2" (5 cm) long. Thin, elongated shrimp-like body, often bent in a loop to move. Clings to eelgrass (p. 93), hydroids (pp. 74–75) and seaweeds, intertidal and shallow subtidal.

Sea Stars, Basket Star & Brittle Star
Phylum Echinodermata

The echinoderms ("spiny-skinned") animals have a variety of shapes (sea stars, sea urchins, sand dollars, sea lilies) but consistently have radial symmetry; adults have 5-part symmetry. They are foragers of live and dead animals, seaweed drift and bottom sediments, and as such they play an important role in marine ecology.

Sea stars

Most sea stars have 5 symmetrical arms (or "rays"), but the number varies by species. The animal has cylindrical tube feet on the underside of each arm, which it uses for locomotion, and a mouth on the underside.

Ochre Star
Pisaster ochraceus
Radius to 10" (25 cm). Thick, stiff body; 5 arms. Purple or orange with network of white spines. Feeds on mussels, barnacles, limpets and snails. Often found in clusters, in tidepools to 290' (87 m) deep.

Pink Star
Pisaster brevispinus
Radius to 12½" (32 cm). Large, stiff body; 5 long arms. Pink to grey. Feeds on bivalves and snails. On soft surfaces, intertidal to 420' (128 m) deep.

Mottled Star
Evasterias troschelii
Radius to 11.8" (30 cm). Small disc; 5 long, tapered arms. Colour variable from rust to brown, orange and blue-grey. Eats a variety of bivalves, chitons, barnacles and sea squirts (pp. 85–86). On rocks or cobble, intertidal to 246' (75 m) deep.

Painted Star
Orthasterias koehleri
Radius to 10" (25 cm). 5 long arms with prominent white or purple spines, reddish banding and white-cream patches. Often feeds on bivalves. On sand–shell to rock, intertidal to 755' (230 m) deep.

Vermilion Star
Mediaster aequalis
Radius to 4" (10 cm). Large, flat disc; 5 tapered arms. Surface covered with vermilion plates. On rocks, intertidal to 961' (293 m) deep.

Six Ray Star
Leptasterias spp.
Radius to 2" (5 cm). Highly variable and difficult to identify as individual species. 6 arms, broad at the base, tapering quickly to blunt tips. Colour varies from grey to green, pink, purple and orange. Under rocks and in crevices, intertidal to 150' (45 m) deep.

Bat Star
Pateria miniata
Radius to 4" (10 cm). Rough, granular surface; 5 short arms with web-footed appearance. Colourful with red, blue, yellow, green and brown. On rocks or sand–mud on exposed coast, intertidal to 991' (302 m) deep.

Leather Star
Dermasterias imbricata
Radius to 6" (15 cm). Smooth, slick, leathery surface; 5 short, thick arms. Upper surface grey with patches of red, brown and purple. On rocks, intertidal to 300' (90 m) deep. Shown here feeding on orange sea pen.

Cookie Star

Ceramaster patagonicus

Radius to 3¼″ (8 cm). Pentagonal disc; 5 short, pointed arms. Slightly inflated. Granular surface with marginal plates. Cream to orange. On rocks to mud, subtidal, 33–804′ (10–245 m) deep.

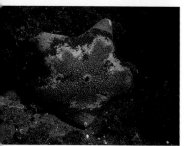

Cushion Star

Pteraster tesselatus

Radius to 4¾″ (11.8 cm). Broad disc; 5 short, stubby arms. Slightly elevated central pore on topside, rather than sieve plate. Yellow to tan and grey, sometimes with pattern. On rocks, subtidal, 20–1,430′ (6–436 m) deep.

Fat Blood Star

Henricia sanguinolenta

Radius to 9¼″ (23 cm). Long, tapered arms, fat and creased where they leave the disc. Nearly white, lavender or pale orange. On rocks to mud, subtidal, 50–1,700′ (15–528 m) deep.

Rose Star

Crossaster papposus

Radius to 7″ (17.5 cm). Soft bodied; 8–16 arms. Purple body with concentric rings of red, orange, white or yellow. On rocks, intertidal to 3,937′ (1,200 m) deep.

Wrinkled Star

Pteraster militaris

Radius to 3″ (7.5 cm). Soft, fleshy wrinkled body with large upper central pore. Cream to yellow to pink. Feeds on sponges and hydrocorals (p. 67). On rocks to mud, subtidal, 30–3,609′ (9–1,100 m) deep.

Blood Star

Henricia leviuscula

Radius to 6¼" (16 cm). Long, thin arms from small disc; 3 rows of plates along lower side of each arm. Orange to brick red, sometimes with grey patch. On rocks, intertidal to 1,435' (431 m) deep.

Spiny Red Star

Hippasteria phrygiana

Radius to 6 5/8" (17 cm). Broad disc; 5 short arms with prominent tapering spines over the body. Red to orange. Feeds on orange sea pens (p. 68) and anemones. On rocks, sand to shell, subtidal, 33–1,680' (10–512 m) deep.

Spiny Mudstar

Luidia foliolata

Radius to 12" (30 cm). Small disc; 5 long, flattened arms with white marginal spines. Dull grey-brown, underside with yellow-orange tube feet. In sand–mud, intertidal to 2,011' (613 m) deep.

Long Ray Star

Stylasterias forreri

Radius to 13" (32.5 cm). Small disc with very long arms. Black or grey with grey wreaths of pincers and white spines. On rocks to sand–mud, 20–1,745' (6–523 m) deep.

Sunflower Star ▼

Pycnopodia helianthoides

Radius to 18" (45 cm). Soft body, broad disc; up to 24 arms. Abundant surface spines, pincers and gills. Fast-moving. On many surfaces, intertidal to 1,435' (431 m) deep. Many sunflower stars were lost to Sea Star Wasting Disease.

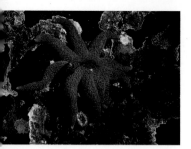

Striped Sunstar
Solaster stimpsoni
Radius to 10" (25 cm). Typically 10, sometimes 9 long, slim, tapering arms. Each arm has a dark purple stripe bordered by blue, pink, red or orange. On rocks and other surfaces, intertidal to 2,000' (600 m) deep.

Morning Sunstar
Solaster dawsoni
Radius to 8" (20 cm). Broad disc; 8–15 long, tapering arms. Brown-orange, occasionally red or mottled brown-orange. Often preys on other sea stars. On rocks, gravel and sand, intertidal to 1,380' (414 m) deep.

Basket Star, Brittle Star

Basket Star
Gorgonocephalus eucnemis
To 18" (45 cm) diameter. 5 arms branch repeatedly into hundreds of branchlets. White to tan with pink to orange-red mottling. Subtidal, 33–6,600' (10–1,980 m) deep.

Daisy Brittle Star
Ophiopholis aculeata
Arms to 6" (15 cm), from a small disc, ¾" (2 cm) diameter. Scallop-edged disc. Long, broad arms with blunt spines. Variable colours and patterns of pink, red, orange, blue, green, grey and black. Under rocks or in kelp holdfasts, intertidal to 6,352' (2,000 m) deep.

Sea Urchins, Sea Cucumbers, Feather Star & Sand Dollar
Phylum Echinodermata

Sea Urchins

Red Sea Urchin
Mesocentrotus franciscanus
Shell to 6" (15 cm) diameter, 2" (5 cm) high. Abundant long, sharp spines. Red to purple-black. Juveniles shelter under spines of adults. On rocky shores and kelp beds, intertidal to 410' (125 m) deep.

Green Sea Urchin
Strongylocentrotus droebachiensis
Shell to 3½" (9 cm) diameter, 1½" (3.8 cm) high. Short, crowded spines, equal in length, are pale green, sometimes purple. Dark tube feet. On rocks, intertidal to 3,795' (1,138 m) deep.

Purple Sea Urchin
Strongylocentrotus purpuratus
Shell to 3½" (9 cm) diameter, 1¾" (4.4 cm) high. Short purple spines to 1" (2.5 cm) in the intertidal and 2 3/8" (6 cm) in the subtidal. On exposed rocky coasts, intertidal to 525' (157 m) deep.

Sea Cucumbers

Orange Sea Cucumber
Cucumaria miniata
To 8" (20 cm) long. Elongated orange body with rows of brown tube feet. Head has 10 bushy tentacles of equal length for feeding. Under rocks or in crevices in currents, intertidal to 740' (222 m) deep.

Creeping Pedal Sea Cucumber
Psolus chitonoides
To 2¾" (7 cm) long. Oval, dome-like body with over-lapping plates. Orange, with 10 brilliant orange tentacles. On rocks, intertidal to 810' (243 m) deep.

White Sea Cucumber
Eupentacta quinquesemita
To 4" (10 cm) long. Elongated body. 8 large and 2 smaller tentacles. White body, sometimes yellow or pink at base of tentacles. Between rocks in currents, intertidal to 180' (54 m) deep.

California Sea Cucumber
Apostichopus californicus
To 20" (50 cm) long. Elongated, fleshy appendages, both large and small. Circle of 20 short, bushy feeding tentacles. Body red to mottled brown-red. In a variety of habitats, intertidal to 820' (246 m) deep.

Feather Star or Sea Lily
The animal's 10 feathery arms capture food in the currents. A ring of jointed appendages attach to rocks.

Feather Star
Florometra serratissima
To 10" (25 cm) high. 10 feathery arms radiate from a plate, attached to the rocks by a ring of appendages. Tan to reddish tan. On rock walls, usually in clusters, subtidal, 33–4,108' (10–1,252 m) deep.

Sand Dollar

Sand Dollar (Eccentric)
Dendraster excentricus
To 4" (10 cm) diameter. Flattened body and short spines on both surfaces. Star-shaped series of holes, resembling the petals of a flower, where respiratory tube feet stick out. Lavender-grey, red-brown to purple-black. White shell is often washed up on shore. On sand, intertidal to 130' (39 m) deep.

Corals & Anemones
Phylum Cnidaria

Hydrocorals

The hydrocorals are named for their calcareous skeletons, which resemble those of true corals. They occur in many forms.

Encrusting Hydrocoral
Stylantheca papillosa
Crust to 1/8" (3 mm) thick, to 6" (15 cm) or more across. Thin, hard, smooth colony with small holes occupied by polyps. Often confused with smooth (no holes) coralline algae, pink rock crust (p. 92). Low intertidal to 100' (30 m).

Pink Hydrocoral ▼
Stylaster venustus
To 3" (7.5 cm) high, 3' (1 m) or more diameter. Mass of thickly branching colonies. Rose pink to faded violet branches with white tips. On clean, current-swept rocks, 40–80' (12–24 m) deep.

Sea Pens

Sea pens are octocorals, each polyp with 8 tentacles. They can retract fully into the sea bottom. Sea pens can often be seen in the shallows by divers, or from boats or wharves.

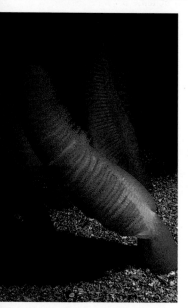

Orange Sea Pen ▼
Ptilosarcus gurneyi
To 18" (45 cm) high, 4" (10 cm) across in spots. Fleshy orange stalk and branches with many polyps. Bioluminescent (glows when disturbed). Anchored in sand–mud, intertidal to 330' (100 m) deep.

Sea Whip
Halipteris willemoesi
To 8' (2.4 m) high, to 3" (7.5 cm) across in spots. Slender, short white branches on a thick supporting rod. In sand–mud, 65' (20 m) and deeper.

White Sea Pen
Virgularia sp.
To 12" (30 cm) high, 4" (10 cm) across in spots. Thin white stalk and slender, delicate white branches. Anchored in sand–mud, 50' (15 m) and deeper. Eaten by the pink tritonia nudibranch (p. 26).

Zoanthids, Cup Corals, Club Anemones

Zoanthids
Epizoanthus scotinus
To 2" (5 cm) high, colonies to at least 3' (1 m) across. Hundreds of orange-yellow individual polyps grow from a common base. On rocks, intertidal and subtidal.

Tan Cup Coral
Caryophyllia alaskensis
To ½" (1 cm) high, 1" (2.5 cm) diameter. Beige or brown to pink polyp with long, slender tentacles. On rocks, shallow subtidal.

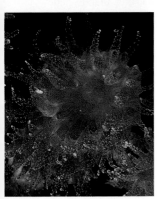

Orange Cup Coral
Balanophyllia elegans
To ½" (1 cm) high, ½" (1 cm) diameter. Solitary calcareous cup, bright orange, polyp with nearly transparent tentacles. On rocks, intertidal to 65' (20 m) deep.

Sea Strawberry Soft Coral
Alcyonium sp.
Lumps to 6" (15 cm) high and wide. Soft, firm colonies of polyps, each an octocoral (has 8 tentacles) with delicate side branches. Cream or pink to red. Eaten by nudibranchs. Juvenile basket stars (p. 64) settle on this coral. On rocks and current-swept areas, rarely intertidal, subtidal to at least 65' (20 m) deep.

Strawberry Anemone
Corynactis californica
To ¾" (2 cm) high, extensive colonies to 65' (20 m) across in spots. Divides to form colony of white to pink, lavender to red bodies, white knobs at tips of tentacles. On current-swept rocks, intertidal to at least 150' (45 m).

Sea Anemones

Giant (Frilled) Plumose Anemone
Metridium farcimen (=M. giganteum)
To 3' (1 m) high, 12" (30 cm) diameter. Smooth column, lobed oral disc with more than 200 slender, translucent tentacles. White, brown or tan to orange. Dense aggregations on floats and rocks, intertidal to 1,000' (300 m) deep.

Plumose Anemone
Metridium senile
To 4" (10 cm) high, 2" (5 cm) diameter. Oral disc not lobed; fewer than 100 slender tentacles grow from it. White, tan to brown, orange. Dense aggregations on rocks and floats, intertidal to 1,000' (300 m) deep.

Aggregate Green Anemone ▼
Anthopleura elegantissima
To 6" (15 cm) high, 3" (7.5 cm) diameter. Budding colonies. Green beaded column, pale green tentacles with pink tips, shown here open and closed (B). On rocks or in current, intertidal and shallow subtidal.

Giant Green Anemone
Anthopleura xanthogrammica
To 12" (30 cm) high, 10" (25 cm) diameter. Column green to olive, tentacles and oral disc uniform green from algae living symbiotically in the tissues. On open coast, intertidal, tidepools and shallow subtidal.

Buried Moonglow Anemone
Anthopleura artemisia
To 10" (25 cm) high, 4" (10 cm) diameter. Column mostly buried. Long, slender tentacles, pink, orange or luminous green-grey, with white bands. In sand, intertidal to 35' (10 m) deep.

Brooding Anemone
Epiactis prolifera
To 4" (10 cm) high, 2" (5 cm) diameter. Low, squat. Vertical white lines on column and radiating lines on disk. Colour varies from pink to green, brown and orange. Young anemones exit mouth; up to 30 young are fixed on the column. Intertidal to 30' (9 m) deep.

Swimming Anemone
Stomphia didemon
To 4" (10 cm) high, 5" (12.5 cm) diameter. Cream to orange, sometimes mottled column with orange, white or banded tentacles. Swims to escape the leather star (p. 61). On rocks, subtidal to 65' (20 m) deep.

Fish-Eating Anemone ▼
Urticina piscivora
To 10" (25 cm) high, 8" (20 cm) diameter. Tall, smooth red-maroon column. Long, slender white, red or pink tentacles, banded on rare occasions. On rocks on open coast, 20–100' (6–30 m) deep.

White-Spotted Anemone
Cribrinopsis albopunctata
To 6" (15 cm) high and wide. Squat scarlet column with vertical rows of white tubercles (projections). Long yellow tentacles with pink tips. On exposed rocky coasts, intertidal to 50' (15 m) deep.

Sand-Rose Anemone
Urticina columbiana
To 10" (25 cm) high, 14" (35 cm) diameter. Column, partially buried in sand, has irregular patches of rough white tubercles. Long, slender, white to pink tentacles. In sand–mud–shell, subtidal to 150' (45 m) or deeper.

Snakelock Anemone
Cribrinopsis rubens
Column to 8" (20 cm) high, with longitudinal rows of tubercles, 6" (15 cm) diameter. Long, slender, drooping tentacles with distinctive raised zigzag lines. White to pink to red. Candystripe and broken back shrimp (p. 55) live under canopy of tentacles. On rocks, subtidal to 1,000' (300 m) deep.

Painted Anemone
Urticina grebelnyi
To 5" (12.5 cm) high, 3" (7.5 cm) diameter. Column variable in colour, with green, red and yellow patches. Rings of short, thick, coloured or banded tentacles, about 100 in all. On rocks, intertidal and shallow subtidal.

Stubby Buried Anemone
Urticina clandestina
To 6" (15 cm) high and wide. Red column, usually partially buried in sand–mud. Green to olive disc has short, blunt, banded tentacles of green, pink, red or blue. Intertidal to 50' (15 m) deep.

Tube-Dwelling Anemone ▼
Pachycerianthus fimbriatus
To 14" (35 cm) long, crown to 8" (20 cm) diameter. Secretes mucus-like tube to 3' (1 m) long in mud. 2 sets of golden brown to purple or black tentacles; short inner circle of tentacles over mouth. Eaten by nudibranchs. Intertidal to 100' (30 m).

Hydroids, Jellyfish & Comb Jellies
Phylum Cnidaria, Phylum Ctenophora

Hydroids
The hydroid is a small animal, which consists of a stalk crowned with a ring of tentacles. Individuals form colonies that resemble bushy plants. A variety of nudibranchs (sea slugs) feed on hydroids.

Pink Mouth Hydroid
Ectopleura marina
To 3" (7.5 cm) high. Solitary. Orange-pink polyp on slender stalk. On rocks and floats, intertidal to 50' (15 m) deep.

Pink Heart Hydroid
Ectopleura crocea
To 5" (12.5 cm) high, colonies more than 12" (30 cm) across. Tangles of straw-like stems; pink and red polyps with grape-like clusters of reproductive organs. On rocks, intertidal to 50' (15 m).

Ostrich Plume Hydroid
Aglaophenia struthionides
To 5" (12.5 cm) high. Polyps are on one side of each feather-like branch (visible only by close inspection, not in photo). Elongated yellow eggs on plumes. On rocks, intertidal to 525' (157 m) deep.

Sea Fir
Abietinaria sp.
To 6" (15 cm) high. Fern-like stem and branches. Polyps on both sides of branches. On rocks, intertidal to 60' (18 m).

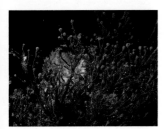

Snail Fur
Hydractinia milleri
To 1/8" (3 mm) high, mats to 2" (5 cm) diameter. Pink, fuzzy mass, joined at the base in a mat that unites the colony. Grows on shells inhabited by hermit crabs (pp. 53–54), shells of crabs and occasionally rocks. Stinging capsules may deter predators. Intertidal to 80' (24 m).

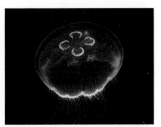

Orange Hydroid
Garveia annulata
To 6" (15 cm) high. Clusters to 12" (30 cm) across of bright orange stems and polyps. On rocks, kelp and sponges, intertidal to 400' (120 m) deep.

Jellyfish

Moon Jelly
Aurelia labiata
To 3" (7.5 cm) high, 8" (20 cm) diameter. 4 horseshoe gonads visible in clear, grey to blue-tinged bell. Bell scalloped into 8 pairs of lobes. Short marginal tentacles. In coastal waters, bays and harbours.

Sail Jellyfish
Velella velella
To 3" (7.5 cm) long. Jellyfish-like hydroid colony. Dark blue-purple, with an upright triangular sail (A). Floats on the surface. A large number of these jellyfish are often blown onto the beaches (B) on the outer coast.

Sea Blubber

Cyanea capillata

Typically to 20" (50 cm); northern specimens to 7' (2 m) diameter. Trailing tentacles to 30' (9 m). 8 pairs of lobes around edge of bell. Red-brown to yellow, rose to white body. Tentacles cause stinging and burning. In coastal waters, bays and harbours.

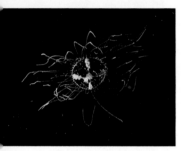

Clinging Jellyfish

Gonionemus vertens

To 1¼" (6 mm) diameter. Jellyfish-like hydroid colony. Transparent bell contains cross-shaped gonads coloured red or orange, to brown or violet. Long tentacles have adhesive pads. Attached to kelp and eelgrass in intertidal and shallow subtidal.

Comb jellies

Phylum Ctenophora

These jellyfish-like animals have sticky cells on their tentacles, rather than stinging cells, which they use to capture food.

Cat's Eye Comb Jelly

Pleurobrachia bachei

To ½" (1 cm) high, 2 trailing tentacles 6" (15 cm) or longer. Round to egg-shaped body with combs (rows of cilia) in a rainbow of colours. In shallow waters, spring to autumn. Often washed ashore (B).

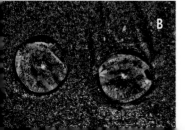

Sponges
Phylum Porifera

Sponges are small animals that feed by filtering water through pores and chambers (Porifera means "hole bearers"). Individuals grow in colonies that range in form from thin mats and crusts to erect tube-like, vase-like or branching masses. The support structure may be calcareous (containing calcium carbonate), or made of siliceous spicules (pointed glass protrusions) or spongin, a tough protein network. Sponges are common on rocks, floats and pilings; intertidal to great depths. They are eaten by nudibranchs (sea slugs), some snails and sea stars.

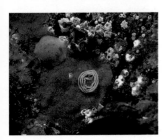

Tube Sponge
Leucosolenia nautilia
Tubes to 1/8" (3 mm) diameter, forming loose branching colonies to 2–6" (5–15 cm) diameter. Calcareous. On rocks and floats, intertidal and shallow subtidal.

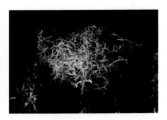

Velvety Red Sponge
Clathria pennata
Thin crust to ¼" (6 mm) thick, to 3' (1 m) diameter. Smooth patches. Coral red, red-brown to mustard colour. Often found with red nudibranch (p. 23) feeding and laying a ribbon of eggs. On rocks, intertidal to 295' (90 m) deep.

Purple Sponge
Haliclona permollis
Encrusting to 1 5/8" high, 3' (1 m) diameter. Raised volcano-like oscula (pores). Pink or lavender to purple. Often eaten by leopard dorid nudibranch (p. 23). On rocks, intertidal.

Yellow Boring Sponge
Cliona californica
Encrusting as yellow spots, patches or masses on shells, protruding from holes to 1/8" (3 mm) diameter. Bores into shells, particularly rock scallop (p. 34) and barnacle (pp. 57–58); sometimes on rocks. Low intertidal to 400' (120 m) deep.

Bread Crumb Sponge
Halichondria panicea
Encrusting to 2" (5 cm) high, 12" (30 cm) or more diameter. Prominent low, volcano-like oscula (pores). Yellow to green. When broken, smells like exploded gunpowder. On rocks and floats, intertidal and shallow subtidal.

Rough Encrusting (Scallop) Sponge
Myxilla (Myxilla) incrustans
Encrusting to 3/8" (9 mm) thick on shell of spiny pink scallop (p. 35). Gold to light brown, with lumpy oscula (pores). Often eaten by nudibranchs. On swimming scallops, 3–500' (1–150 m) deep.

Smooth Encrusting (Scallop) Sponge
Mycale (Aegograpila) adhaerens
Encrusting to 3/8" (9 mm) thick on shell of spiny pink scallop (p. 35). Yellow-brown to violet. Smoother and smaller oscula (pores) than rough encrusting sponge. On swimming scallops, 3–500' (1–150 m) deep.

Hermit Crab Sponge ▼
Suberites latus
Encrusting lumps to 3" (7.5 cm) high and wide. Settles on and dissolves shells inhabited by hermit crabs. Grey, brown to dark orange. Hermit crabs grow within the growing sponge and do not need to fight for larger shells. Low intertidal to 120' (36 m) deep.

Western Nipple Sponge

Polymastia pachymastia

Mat to ¼" (6 mm) thick, 12" (30 cm) diameter. Many raised nipple-like oscula (pores) to 3/8" (9 mm) high. Cream-yellow. On rocks, intertidal to 600' (180 m) deep.

Cloud Sponge

Aphrocallistes vastus

Large, erect, to 6½' (2 m) high, branching growths to 10' (3 m) diameter. Siliceous with 6-rayed spicules (pointed projections). On rocks in inlets, 80' (24 m) and deeper.

Chimney (Boot) Sponge ▼

Rhabdocalyptus dowlingi

Large tube to 5' (1.5 m) high, 3' (1 m) diameter. Siliceous, with 6-rayed spicules (pointed projections). Lip is rounded. Sediment is trapped in body bristles. Stands on rocks, 40' (12 m) and deeper.

Tennis Ball Sponge

Craniella villosa

Globular, to 6" (15 cm) diameter. Grey exterior with a ridge and holes on top; white to yellow interior. On rocks, intertidal to 65' (20 m) deep.

Orange Puffball Sponge

Tethya californiana

Globular, to 6" (15 cm) diameter. Rough surface with many ostia (small pores). Orange or yellow to green in colour. On rocks, often in muddy areas, 20' (6 m) and deeper.

Worms
Phylum Annelida, Phylum Nemertea,
Phylum Platyhelminthes

Segmented Worms
Phylum Annelida
The bodies of these worms are divided into obvious segments by encircling grooves. They may have bristles or paddle-like appendages. A segmented worm may be free-moving, or burrowing, or fixed in a tube with only the head visible, modified as a plume.

Northern Feather Duster Worm
Eudistylia vancouveri
Tube to 2' (60 cm) high, ½" (1 cm) diameter; worm to 6" (15 cm) diameter, plume to 2" (5 cm) across. Distinctive banded green and maroon plumes protrude from long, light grey or brown parchment-like tubes. On rocks and floats, intertidal to 65' (20 m).

Calcareous Tube Worm
Serpula columbiana
Tube to 4" (10 cm) long, ¼" (6 mm) diameter; worm to 4" (10 cm) long; plume to ¾" (2 cm) diameter. White, rambling, limy tubes. Tentacles red, sometimes banded with white. Conical stoppers close off tube as worm withdraws. Tubes attached to rocks, pilings or floats, often on underside, intertidal to at least 330' (100 m).

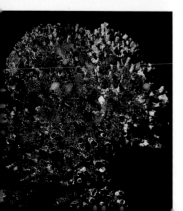

Fringed Tube Worm
Dodecaceria fewkesi
Tubes to 1 5/8" (4 cm) long, 1/8" (3 mm) wide, in clumps to 3' (1 m) diameter. Short, hard, limy tube. Dark brown or green to black body with 11 pairs of dark filaments growing from head. On rocks, intertidal to 65' (20 m).

Pacific Lugworm and Castings
Abarenicola pacifica
To 6" (15 cm) long. A burrowing worm found near coiled pile of castings. Green to red body, red gills when wet. On sand–mud beaches, high intertidal.

Mussel (Pile) Worm ▼
Nereis vexillosa
To 12" (30 cm) long. Many large paddle-like feet. Dark, iridescent green, blue and grey. Everts pincer-like jaws to feed. Free-moving in mussel beds or mud–gravel of clam beds, or burrowed in sand–mud–gravel, intertidal and shallow subtidal.

Scale Worm
Halosydna brevisetosa
To 2 3/8" (6 cm) long. Slender, brown-grey body with 18 pairs of black-spotted scales along back. Free-living on floats, in mussel beds or under rocks, intertidal to 1,790' (540 m).

Ribbon Worms

Phylum Nemertea

These worms have long, thin, somewhat flattened bodies that are not segmented. They are found under rocks and in barnacle clumps, mussel beds and kelp hold-fasts. The ribbon worm attacks its prey with a proboscis, a long feeding apparatus that shoots out from the head.

Green and Yellow Ribbon Worm

Emplectonema gracile

To 4" (10 cm) long and 1/16" (2 mm) wide. Dark green on top, yellowish green below. Under rocks, in barnacle clusters, in mussel beds, intertidal.

Orange Ribbon Worm

Tubulanus polymorphus

To 10" (25 cm) long, 3/16" (5 mm) wide. Thin, often coiled body with broad, rounded head. Bright orange. Under rocks, intertidal to 165' (50 m) deep.

Flatworms

Phylum Platyhelminthes

The flatworms have flattened oval bodies. They are free-moving, and are usually seen under rocks, in mussel beds and in tunicates (see p.87).

Giant Flatworm

Kaburakia excelsa

To 4" (10 cm) long, 2¾" (7 cm) wide, 1/8" (3 mm) thick. Firm oval body. 2 short tentacles with eye spots. Orange to brown, spotted. Under rocks and in mussel beds, intertidal.

Other Small Marine Animals
Moss Animals (Bryozoans), Sea Squirts & Tunicates

Moss Animals (Bryozoans)
Phylum Bryozoa
These tiny animals live in colonies that resemble moss. Tiny individuals are cased in box-like or tube-like units of limy, calcareous or other stiff material. A crown of fringed tentacles protrudes from each pore. The animals often divide to reproduce.

Staghorn Bryozoan
Heteropora pacifica
Colony to 2" (5 cm) high, to 6" (15 cm) diameter. Greenish branches, not joined, with rounded yellow tips. On rocks, subtidal to 90' (27 m) deep.

Kelp Lacy Bryozoan (Lacy Crust)
Membranipora spp.
Thin, lacy crusts to 3" (7.5 cm) diameter. Silver patches of small intersecting "boxes." On kelp, floats and rocks, shallow subtidal. Identification requires microscopic examination.

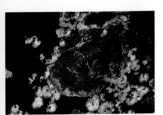

Orange Crust Bryozoan
Schizoporella unicornis
Thin crust to 2" (5 cm) diameter. Orange, brown or golden with fine pattern of pores. On rocks, shells, floats and kelp, intertidal to 200' (60 m) deep. Introduced from Japan.

Spiral Bryozoan
Bugulina californica
One or more spirals to 2¾" (7 cm) high. Branches grow in whorls, whitish tan to orange. On rocks and shells, shallow subtidal to 1,320' (400 m) deep.

Sculptured Bryozoan
Primavelans insculpta
To 4" (10 cm) high, 4" (10 cm) diameter. Layered frills with double-fluted branches, yellow-tan to orange. On rocks, subtidal to 770' (230 m) deep.

Lacy Bryozoan
Phidolopora pacifica
To 2½" (5 cm) high, 8½" (21 cm) diameter. Stiff, brittle, ruffled formation, salmon pink to orange or white. Shown here with purple-ring topsnail (p. 41). On rocks, intertidal to 660' (200 m) deep.

Stick Bryozoan
Microprella borealis
To 4" (10 cm) high, 4" (10 cm) diameter. Short, jointed segments, elliptical in cross-section. Yellow-cream to tan. On rocks, shallow subtidal to 1,320' (400 m) deep.

White Branching Bryozoan
Diaperoforma californica
Masses to 1" (2.5 cm) high and 10" (25 cm) across in spots. White to dark yellow, flattened branches. On rocks, shells and giant kelps, subtidal to 600' (180 m) deep.

Smooth Leather Bryozoan
Alcyonidium pendunculatum
To 4" (10 cm) high, 2" (5 cm) across in spots. Flattened leathery branches, tan with short brown spines along the edges. On rocks and shells, intertidal to 245' (73 m) deep.

Sea Squirts, Tunicates (Compound Ascidians)
Phylum Urochordata
These colourful, jelly-like animals resemble sponges. Each individual has 2 siphons to pump water through the body. Colonies often carpet floats and the seafloor. Individuals may be solitary in form (sea squirts), or occur in aggregations or compound ascidian colonies (tunicates, so-called because individuals are embedded in a common skin-like tunic).

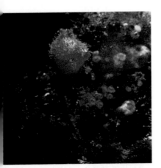

Stalked Hairy Sea Squirt
Boltenia villosa
To 1 5/8" (4 cm) high, 1¼" (3 cm) wide. Solitary. Stalk with red-orange, tan to brown tunic, covered with hairs or spines. Low intertidal to 330' (99 m) deep.

Stalked Sea Squirt
Styela montereyensis
To 10" (25 cm) high. Solitary. Long, thin stalk, grooved, with 2 siphons at the tip, one straight and one bent over. Orange-red to brown. In currents, on rocks, intertidal to 100' (30 m) deep.

Sea Peach
Halocynthia aurantium
To 6" (15 cm) high. Solitary. Smooth and barrel-shaped with large projecting siphons. Orange-red. On rocks, subtidal to 330' (99 m) deep.

Smooth Orange Sea Squirt

Cnemidocarpa finmarkiensis

To 3" (7.5 cm) high, 2" (5 cm) diameter. Solitary. Smooth, squat, pearly orange-red tunic. Two short projecting siphons. On rocks, intertidal to 165' (50 m) deep.

Wrinkled Sea Squirt

Pyura haustor

To 3" (7.5 cm) high, 3" (7.5 cm) diameter. Solitary. Distinctive long, slender red-pink siphons protrude from warty base. In clusters, on rocks, intertidal to 660' (200 m) deep.

Glassy Sea Squirt

Ascidia paratropa

To 6" (15 cm) high. Solitary. Clear cylindrical tunic with obvious fleshy spines, prominent siphons. On rocks, in current areas, intertidal to 265' (80 m) deep.

Spiny Sea Squirt

Halocynthia igaboja

To 4" (10 cm) high, 4" (10 cm) diameter. Globular, spiny body, often grey-black with silt. Reddish siphons close to form a cross shape. On rocks, intertidal to 540' (162 m) deep.

Light Bulb Ascidian

Clavelina huntsmani

To 2" (5 cm) high, clusters to 20" (50 cm) across. Colonial. Transparent tubes, each with 2 orange-pink "filaments." On rocks, subtidal to 100' (30 m) deep.

Orange Social Ascidians
Metandrocarpa taylori
To ¼" (6 mm) high. Clustered individuals joined by a slender stolon (stem-like structure) or thin tunic sheet. On rocks, in currents, intertidal to 65' (20 m) deep.

Lobed Ascidian
Cystodytes lobatus
To 1½" (3.8 cm) thick, patches to 10" (25 cm) or more diameter. Encrusting colony with irregular ridges and lobes. Grey or purple-pink. On exposed coasts, on rocks, intertidal to 660' (200 m) deep.

Sea Pork
Aplidium californicum
To 1¾" (4.4 cm) thick, 12" (30 cm) across. Encrusting sheets. Yellow, grey, opalescent white or transparent colonies. On rocks, in current or wave-exposed areas, intertidal to 280' (85 m) deep.

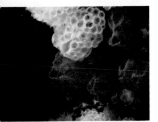

Mushroom Ascidian
Distaplia occidentalis
To 1½" (3.8 cm) high, 4" (10 cm) across. Colonies, mushroom-shaped to flattened, rounded. Variable colours from white to grey, yellow, pink, red, or purple-brown. On rocks, in currents or surge, intertidal to 50' (15 m) deep.

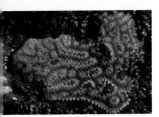

Chain (Lined) Compound Tunicate
Botrylloides violaceus
Thin sheet, 1/8" (3 mm) thick, colonies to 6" (15 cm) and more across on hard surfaces. Colony organized in elongated rows, usually one solid colour, purple, pink, yellow, orange or white. Intertidal to 165' (50 m). Japanese.

Harbour Star Compound Tunicate
Botryllus schlosseri
Thin sheet, 1/8" (3 mm) thick, colonies to 6" (15 cm) and more across on hard surfaces. Colony organized in star or flower-shaped patterns, often two-toned, strong colour orange, black, brown or green. Intertidal to 660' (200 m). Introduced, Atlantic–Med. Sea.

Seaweeds & Seagrasses

There may be as many as 700 species of seaweeds, microscopic algae and sea grasses along the Pacific Coast from Alaska to California.

Green Seaweeds
Phylum Chlorophyta
These seaweeds, typically grass green or olive green, grow in shallow waters. Most species are less than 12" (30 cm) long, including filaments, blades, cylinders, spongy mats and spheres.

Sea Lettuce
Ulva spp.
To 7" (17.5 cm) long and wide. Thin blades, often with ruffled or incised edges. Small, distinct stipe (stem). Bright green. Common, but difficult to identify positively in habitat. Along protected shores, mid- to low intertidal.

Sea Hair (Tubeweed)
Ulva spp.
To 8" (20 cm) long, to ¼" (6 mm) diameter. Stringy mats, yellow-green to dark green. Difficult to identify positively in habitat. Free-floating in tidepools, attached to rocks in high to mid-intertidal.

Sea Staghorn
Codium fragile
To 16" (40 cm) high. Sponge-like, branching growths. Dark green. In tidepools and among rocks, mid- to low intertidal.

Green Spongy Cushion
Codium setchellii
To ¾" (2 cm) thick and 10" (25 cm) diameter. Sponge-like, shiny dark green patches. Low intertidal.

Green Tuft
Cladophora sp.
To 2" (5 cm) high and 12" (30 cm) diameter. Bright green filamentous tufts. On rocks along exposed to protected shores, mid- to low intertidal.

Brown Seaweeds
Phylum Ocrophyta, Class Phaeophyceae
These are the largest and most visible seaweeds on the coast. They range in colour from olive green to dark brown to almost black. The brown seaweeds occur as crusts, filaments, globular, flat-bladed, branched-bladed, feather-like and ribbed forms.

Rockweed
Fucus distichus
Flattened branches to 20" (50 cm) long. Midrib on olive green to yellow-brown branches; swollen terminal ends. On rocks, mid- to low intertidal.

Little Rockweed
Pelvetiopsis limitata
To 3¼" (8 cm) tall. Flattened stems without midribs; swollen terminal ends. Light tan to olive. On rocks, high intertidal.

Sea Cauliflower ▼
Leathesia marina
To 1" (2.5 cm) tall, 5" (12.5 cm) diameter. Convoluted and globular. Yellowish brown to golden. Attached to rocks, mid-intertidal.

Bull Kelp ▼

Nereocystis luetkeana

Single stalk to 65′ (20 m) long. Float (reproductive part) to 5″ (12.5 cm) diameter. Broad, flat blades to 10′ (3 m) long, 8″ (20 cm) wide. Olive to dark brown. Attached by holdfast to rocks, forming kelp beds on protected to exposed shores, lowest intertidal to 65′ (20 m) deep.

Small Perennial Kelp (Northern Giant Kelp) ▼

Macrocystis pyrifera

To 99′ (30 m) long. Flattened holdfast (a feature that distinguishes this species from a similar one). Numerous branches, slit blades and pear-shaped floats (reproductive parts) form extensive canopies. Olive to dark brown. In sheltered waters along the open coast, lowest intertidal to 33′ (10 m) deep.

Wireweed (Sargassum)

Sargassum muticum

To 10′ (3 m) tall. Short stock, branching repeatedly, spherical floats (reproductive parts). Introduced from Japan. Attached to rocks or shells, low intertidal to 16′ (5 m) deep. Introduced from Japan.

Sea Palm
Postelsia palmaeformis
To 2' (60 cm) tall. Stubby holdfast. Long, flexible stalk with numerous drooping blades to 10" (25 cm) long. Greenish to olive-brown. On surf-exposed rocks, mid- to low intertidal.

Feather Boa
Egregia menziesii
To 65' (20 m) long. Strap-like stem, densely covered with blades and elongated floats to 2" (5 cm) long. Olive to dark brown. On exposed coasts, intertidal to 65' (20 m) deep.

Red Seaweeds
Phylum Rhodophyta
The red seaweeds live at greater depths than others. Colours range from shades of red and brown to purple and black. Species occur in encrusting patches, in a filamentous form, or in large, conspicuous blades that may be smooth or ribbed.

Purple Laver
Pyropia perforata
To 12" (30 cm) long and wide. Tiny, disc-shaped holdfast. Thin, broad, delicate, lobed or ruffled blade. Iridescent purple to purple-green. On rocks, mussels and other algae along protected and exposed shores, upper to mid-intertidal.

Turkish Towel
Chondracanthus exasperatus
To 16" (40 cm) long. Broad, thick, unbranched blades, bearing stiff projections. Brick red to shades of purple, iridescent when wet. The most common of several similar species. On intertidal rocks and subtidal to 65' (20 m).

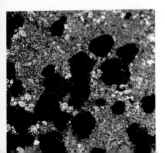

Nail Brush
Endocladia muricata
To 3" (7.5 cm) tall. Dense, stiff, bushy clumps of cylindrical branches. Pinkish or dark red to black-brown. On rocks and mussels along exposed shores, upper to mid-intertidal.

Black Pine

Neorhodomela larix

To 12" (30 cm) long. Wiry branches with small clusters of ringlets. Dark brown-black. Coarse mats on sandy, rocky reefs, upper to low intertidal.

Sea Sac

Halosaccion glandiforme

To 6" (15 cm) long, ¾" (2 cm) wide. Groups of finger-like sacs. Bright purple-red to pale yellow. On rocks, in a band along exposed and transition shores, mid-intertidal.

Coralline Algae

The NE Pacific has a greater diversity of corallines than anywhere else in the world.

Pink Rock Crust (Coralline Algae)

There are many species in several genera (e.g. Callilithophyum, Crusticorallina) with numerous recent name changes.

To 1/8" (3 mm) thick, often round to 4" (10 cm) diameter. Smooth or covered with bumps. Pink. Common, but difficult to identify positively without microscopic examination and DNA analysis. On rocks and shells, intertidal to 33' (10 m).

Branching Coralline Algae

Many species in several genera, including Bossiella, Calliarthron, Corallina and others, with numerous recent name changes.

To at least 6" (15 cm) tall. Flattened branches with jointed segments. Common, but difficult to identify positively without microscopic examination and in some cases, DNA analysis. In tidepools, lower intertidal, shallow subtidal.

Seagrasses
Phylum Anthophyta

These rooted aquatic seed plants form important, productive shoreline habitats for many fishes and marine animals. They are not true grasses but flowering plants related to lilies.

Dwarf Eelgrass
Zostera japonica

Thin, short blades to 8" (20 cm) long, less than 1/8" (3 mm) wide. Dark green. Introduced from Japan. Along wave-protected shores, intertidal, higher on beach than native eelgrass.

(Scouler's) Surfgrass
Phyllospadix scouleri

Flat, narrow blades to 3' (90 cm) long, to 1/8" (3 mm) wide. Bright emerald green. Attached to intertidal rocks on surf-exposed shores.

Eelgrass
Zostera marina

Flat blades to 4' (1.2 m) long, ¼" (6 mm) wide. Dull green. Rooted in sand and mud in wave-protected areas, low intertidal to shallow subtidal, at least 33' (10 m) deep. Shown here coated with herring spawn.

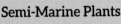

Semi-Marine Plants
Phylum Anthophyta

Sea Asparagus (Pickleweed)
Sarcoconia pacifica

Spreading, branching mats to 10" (25 cm) tall. Along protected shores, tide flats and salt-water marshes, high intertidal.

List of Species